THE
NEW BEETLE

WOB·NB 88

Matt DeLorenzo

MBI Publishing
Company

First published in 1998 by MBI Publishing Company, 729 Prospect Avenue, PO Box 1, Osceola, WI 54020-0001 USA

MBI Publishing Company books are also available at discounts in bulk quantity for industrial or sales-promotional use. For details write to Special Sales Manager at Motorbooks International Wholesalers & Distributors, 729 Prospect Avenue, PO Box 1, Osceola, WI 54020-0001 USA.

Library of Congress Cataloging-in-Publication Data

DeLorenzo, Matt.
    The New Beetle / Matt DeLorenzo.
        p. cm. -- (Enthusiast color series)
    Includes index.
    ISBN 0-7603-0644-3 (alk. paper)

1. Volkswagen Beetle automobile.
    I. Title. II. Series.
TL215.V6D43   1998
629.222'2--dc21

On the front cover: A car conceived, built and promoted on the basis of a 30 year-old cultural icon? That is exactly the gamble Volkswagen was willing to take on the New Beetle. *Jim Frenak*

On the frontispiece: The New Beetle's designers strove to incorporate elements of the old with the new such as including a fresh twist on the favorite bug-eye styled headlights.

On the title page: A New Beetle meets Volkswagen's original in the Alps' Grossglockner Pass. *Jim Fets*

On the back cover: With the New Beetle, Volkswagen looks ahead to rekindling the nostalgia and identification that the world once felt for one of its cars. *Arni Katz, courtesy of Volkswagen*

On page 96: Spoiler on the 1.8L Turbo. Jim Fets

Edited by John Adams-Graf
Designed by Katie L. Sonmor

Printed in Hong Kong through World Print, Ltd.

Contents

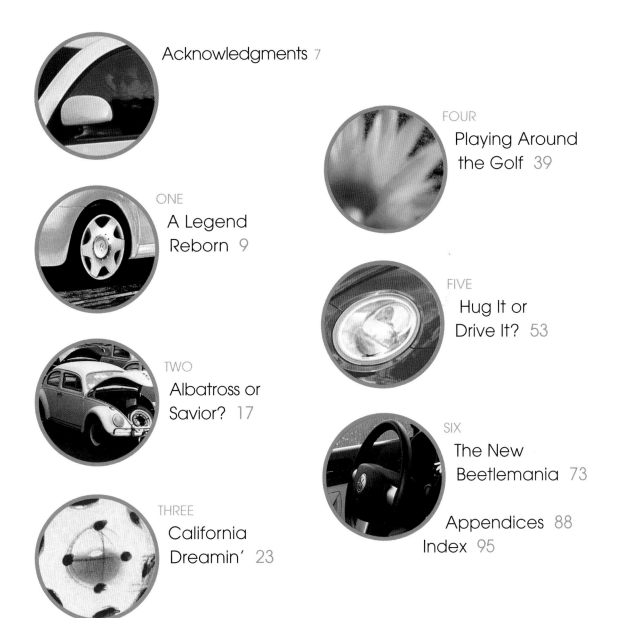

Acknowledgments

This book would not have been possible without the cooperation and candor of the top executives of Volkswagen AG and Volkswagen of America. It would have been easy to say the New Beetle was a great idea from the start and let it go at that, but those running the company had the courage to express their doubts, explain their initial misgivings, and detail the difficulties they had with this project. The result is a remarkable story about a remarkable car.

I'd like to thank Dr. Ferdinand Piëch, chairman of VW AG, for his forthright interviews conducted during a time when the New Beetle was just one concern of many for him. Other VW AG executives who contributed their understanding to this work include Dr. Jens Neumann, Martin Winterkorn, Hartmut Warkuss, and Rudiger Folten. I'd also like to thank designers Freeman Thomas and J. Mays for their cooperation.

Sincere appreciation also goes to the public relations staff at Volkswagen of America, which supplied the many photographs, clips, and speeches and set up key interviews. They include Steve Keyes, Tony Fouladpour, Karla Waterhouse, intern Chris Bokich, and Sue Wogan, editor-in-chief of *Volkwagen Driver* magazine. Also, special thanks to the former public relations director Maria Leonhauser-Rosenau for her insights.

John Love of Event Management was incomparable in pulling together information and resources from the North American International Auto Show. Also helping provide a key interview transcript was Dan McGinn of *Newsweek*, while freelance photographer Joe Wilssens helped track down a few rare shots of the New Beetle.

This work wouldn't have happened without the understanding and forbearance of my boss, Thos. Bryant, editor-in-chief of *Road & Track*.

Finally, I'd like to thank my crack copy editor and wife, Jane, as well as our children, Amy and Stephen, for their patience.

Matt DeLorenzo

Just like its predecessor, the New Beetle attracts attention. Today, however, the New Beetle evokes a sense of nostalgia in addition to the reaction to its styling. *Volkswagen*

A Legend Reborn

Imagine that the original Volkswagen Beetle never existed. What would baby boomers have driven off to college? There'd be no fond remembrances of a car that people could buy new for under $2,000, drive for 100,000 miles, while filling the tank each time for less than two bucks, and then resell for more than half the purchase price. There'd be no tales of improvising roadside repairs, scraping frost off the inside of the windows, or romancing in the confined space of the back seat. There'd be no *Herbie, the Love Bug* movies. Would Woody Allen have gotten as big a laugh in the movie *Sleeper* if he discovered and started a Ford Pinto instead of a Beetle in that cave? Those memorable ads showing that Volkswagens could float or telling us to "Think Small" would've never appeared. California off-roaders would never have invented Dune Buggies. In short, a large chunk of popular culture for several generations of Americans would be missing. The car itself was so unlike any other car—rear-engined, air-cooled, cheap, fairly reliable, and simple-to-maintain—it is unlikely any other manufacturer would, or could, have built one like it.

But there was a Beetle. In fact, there were many of them; some 21 million were built worldwide, and more than a quarter ended up in the United States. The ubiquitous nature of the Beetle contributed to its popularity. They were everywhere. When Volkswagen stopped selling the Beetle in the United States in the mid-1970s, it quickly found itself nowhere. Sales plunged from over a half million units a year in 1970 to less than 40,000 by 1992. And where VW achieved its high watermark with just one car, its paltry sales 20 years later were spread over three models—Golf, Jetta, and Passat. The irony of it was that the Golf hatchback, a flop in the United States, had replaced the Beetle in the rest of the world and was selling well.

Something needed to be done soon or Volkswagen would go the way of other European car companies like Renault, Peugeot, and Fiat and abandon the American market.

That something was a secret project, hatched in VW's newly opened California design studio and approved by just a few high-level executives in Ger-

Artist John Marsh was commissioned by Volkswagen to depict the design process of Concept 1 on canvas. J. Mays and Freeman Thomas are standing just to the right of Concept 1. A cutout of Dr. Ferdinand Porsche, designer of the original Beetle, can be seen to the left of the quarter-scale clay model in the foreground. *Volkswagen*

An early Beetle was a study in simplicity. *Volkswagen*

many, called Concept 1. It would become the New Beetle. In hindsight, the decision to build it looks simple. But at the time it was a huge risk. Despite the approval of the higher-ups in Germany, most Volkswagen top executives were focused on the future. For them, it was as if the Beetle had never existed. But the designers, who still saw Beetles being driven daily in California, were sure that a Beetle-like shape would allow VW to tap into tremendous reserves of goodwill built up by the original car.

The test would be the reaction at the 1994 North American International Auto Show in Detroit: neutral ground for the two camps for a couple of reasons. First, the show attracts international press. Second, it is held in the backyard of the Big Three in a region where Beetles are rare commodities. So it provided the perfect venue for VW to gauge both the response of the automotive media (a relatively jaded lot from around the world) and of a public which probably hadn't seen—much less driven—a Beetle lately.

The hype and hoopla of the Detroit show, where manufacturers routinely engage in games of one-upmanship, would seem daunting to a company looking to refloat its image on the back of a trial balloon. The 1994 show presented some formidable competition, much of it from Chrysler, which launched the Chrysler Cirrus and Dodge Stratus with a *Mission: Impossible*-themed press conference hosted by Peter Graves. Chrysler also introduced the production version of the Neon, a small, round-eyed, huggable subcompact with a base price of under $9,000 that was being touted as the spiritual successor to the original Beetle. If Concept 1 could overcome this juggernaut, it would give VW the push it needed to go forward with the project. If it was greeted with yawns, Concept 1 could be quickly dispatched and VW could move onto other projects.

Secrecy was key. Worried that word of the concept car would leak out, VW's public relations director, Maria Leonhauser, kept the press kits at her home. Show organizers were told that VW would have "something" but weren't told what. Freeman Thomas, one of Concept 1's designers from VW's California studio, drove the heavily disguised show car into Detroit's Cobo Hall. Leonhauser said "it looked like a Fred Flintstone mobile. It had Styrofoam pieces attached to the body that gave it a boxy look. It was covered by a tarp with a slit cut for a window. You could see Freeman peering out as he drove it into the stand."

The stand itself was a large cylinder where the Concept 1 was closed off from prying eyes. A guard was stationed and only a few people were allowed inside before the press conference. Even the head of Volkswagen's sister company, Audi AG, was refused admittance. Worried that no one would attend the VW press conference because of the secrecy surrounding the project (journalists are routinely briefed in advance about what to expect at auto shows), Leonhauser sent out some last-minute postcards inviting the media to the VW press conference to see Concept 1.

Despite all the secrecy, anticipation, and confidence of the U.S. staff that Concept 1 would be a smash hit, the question of how it would be received by the press and public hung heavily in the background.

One year earlier, Porsche had stunned the show with its Boxster concept, a retro-styled concept car that recalled the legendary 550 Spyder. It promised to build the car. Would a retro Beetle be perceived as just a me-too response? Would the press savage Volkswagen, which was already on the ropes in the U.S. market, calling it a desperate move? Would the public care about the Beetle anymore?

Concept 1 would be like no Beetle ever imagined. Mechanically, it would be the complete opposite of the original: front-drive instead of rear-drive, front-engined instead of rear-engined,

Exuberance is a hallmark of the Beetle's role in youth culture. *Volkswagen*

liquid- instead of air-cooled, inline cylinder placement instead of horizontally opposed, a hatchback instead of a two-door. And unlike the spartan original, the New Beetle envisioned by Concept 1 would have air conditioning, airbags, a sound system with a CD player, power steering and brakes, power windows, and a sophisticated microchip-controlled engine management system. A new Beetle would not be cheap. Roadside repairs would be out of the question. The only similarity Concept 1 offered was the shape of the Beetle, a remembrance of things past. Would nostalgia be enough to carry the day?

The Germans didn't think so. Never too impressed with the original Beetle to begin with, many in Volkswagen's technical ranks never worked on the original. They were the types who believed that the best car was talways the next one they were working on. They did not live in the past.

Ullie Seiffert, the board member in charge of technical development, was a member of that breed. He had participated in the safety and emission battles in Washington, D.C. that eventually doomed the original Beetle. He then went on to help develop the Golf that replaced it. The Golf was by now far more important to Volkswagen than the Beetle had ever been. The bad thing was that the Golf, a hatchback, didn't sell well in the United States. So poor were sales that VW had to close the assembly plant it had built in Pennsylvania to supply Golfs and Jettas to North America.

As a result, the Concept 1 press conference, which was held on Wednesday, January 5, 1994, (essentially the last press day of the show), was structured with three distinct elements, any of which could have been emphasized given the response to Concept 1. The first, handled by Thomas Shaver (then head of Volkswagen of America's sales and marketing efforts) touted the third generation Golf and Jetta, which were to be introduced later in the year. Next, Seiffert would introduce the Concept 1. Finally, Seiffert would also emphasize the three alternative-fuel powerplants that Volkswagen was working on to meet future fuel economy and emission regulations. If Seiffert wasn't overly fond of Concept 1, at least he could be enthusiastic about the powerplants a direct-injection turbo-diesel that automatically stops and starts the engine to avoid idling when the vehicle is at rest, a hybrid that combined a diesel with an electric motor powered by nickel/hydride batteries and a pure electric powered by sodium-nickel-chloride batteries.

But from the start, Seiffert was upstaged by Concept 1, almost ambushed by the emotional video concocted by the car's designers. "It's funny the things we remember," the video showed in text. "The things we hang on to. The first day of school. A first dance. A first kiss. Our first car. Some things are simply unforgettable." Shown were stills and videos of old Beetles against swelling violin music. "One little thing can bring it all rushing back. A song on the radio. The smell of suntan lotion. Seeing an old friend at the beach. The friend you could always depend on. Everything was a little less complicated then. Tennis shoes didn't cost $200. A jukebox played your favorite song. And a car was a part of the family. Right from the start." Then the tempo began to change. The music quickened and shots of the Concept 1 began to be shown.

"What if quality never went out of style? What if originality still meant something original? What if simplicity, honesty, and reliability came back again? Imagine a new Volkswagen. A concept that defines the automotive icon. Imagine a vision of high technology and advanced engineering. An expression of innovation, safety, and performance. Imagine the descendent of an enduring original. Different, unmistakable, yet true to its heritage in style and spirit. Every line, every curve, every memory. Not just the evolution of a cherished classic, but the continuation of a worldwide love affair that began 21

Marketing helped establish the Beetle as an alternative to the large cars of the 1960s. This classic Doyle Dane Bernbach ad encourages small thinking. *Volkswagen*

million cars ago. Innovation embodied in tradition. A new Volkswagen concept. One look, and it all comes back. But then, it never really left. The legend reborn. A friendship rekindled."

The cylinder on-stage turned around to reveal Concept 1. Seiffert began stiffly, saying, "Concept 1 is unmistakably a Volkswagen. The intent is to emphasize the typical qualities of a Volkswagen: its honest, reliable, timeless, and youthful design. But Concept 1 is not only interesting from a design viewpoint that combines modern interior space with traditional exterior lines. The true technical advancements of the concept car are found under the hood. This car meets fuel consumption and exhaust emissions standards that address future demands." And then he launched into a technical discussion of the three engines.

Concept 1 captures the simple, friendly shape of the original Beetle. *Volkswagen*

In the question and answer session, Seiffert said, in essence, that there was no plan to build Concept 1, that it was just an idea to gauge public interest. "We can never bring the Beetle back," Seiffert was quoted as saying. "But we would like to go back to our roots with an honest, reliable, timeless, and youthful design on an affordable car." But to the press, that car would be Concept 1—the New Beetle. The reception was enthusiastic. According to Helen Fogel's account of the press conference in the *Detroit News*, the debut "actually brought tears to the eyes of some automotive journalists."

Veteran *Chicago Tribune* automotive reporter Jim Mateja summed up the reaction nicely in his

Concept 1 bows at the North American International Auto Show, January 5, 1994. Ullie Seiffert, who was in charge of the technical development of the car, stands behind the podium at left. *Detroit Auto Dealers Association*

February 13, 1994, column that began with an open letter to Dr. Ferdinand Piëch, the chairman of Volkswagen AG:

Dear Dr. Piëch,

What are you waiting for, Doc? Bring back the Beetle. And hurry.

In case you haven't noticed, VW has been in the latrine since you stopped selling the Beetle in the U.S.

Unless you come up with a new, small, dependable, inexpensive car like the old Beetle real quick, you're going to find that Volkswagen, once a household word, is soon going to be the answer to a Trivial Pursuit question.

You have the opportunity to get what most people in life don't—a second chance to regain the fortune you once enjoyed when the VW Beetle was one of the most popular cars in the universe despite being butt-ugly, cramped, and lacking most of the essentials of vehicle motoring, from gas gauge to radio.

So take a close look at the Concept 1 car that was shipped from your Simi Valley, Calif. design studios. Then let the board of directors give it a glance before you call for the formal vote—All in favor say "*jawohl*" and get on with it. People are waiting.

But not everyone was waiting. Robert Dvorchak, writing for the Associated Press, filed a story in which he spoke to Shell Tomlin, president of the Volkswagen Club of America. Tomlin said the original Beetle was "inexpensive, fun to drive, and easy to maintain. I guess it was ugly, but it ran and ran and ran." Dvorchak said Tomlin was unimpressed by the technology showcased by Concept 1. "We all know those modern things cost money," Tomlin said. "The Concept 1 is not a Beetle. I think people are going to be disappointed in it. I don't know if I would even have one."

There were some very good reasons why the Germans running Volkswagen AG could agree.

TWO

Albatross or Savior?

The reaction to Concept 1 at the North American International Auto Show was not surprising to its designers, J. Mays and Freeman Thomas. As Americans, they made an entirely different connection with the original Beetle than did the German executives running Volkswagen.

The reason for that difference in perception can be summed up in a single word: history. The original Beetle, depending on a person's background, carries with it good and bad emotional baggage. It just depends on how old you are and where you were born.

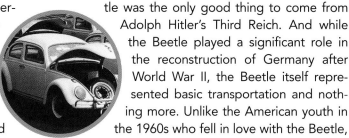

To baby boomers like J. Mays and Freeman Thomas, the Beetle is part of their youth. Even though the Bug was first imported to the United States in 1949, it really wasn't "invented" for a good many Americans until the 1960s, when boomers started getting their licenses and were looking for cheap, reliable transportation (with more emphasis on cheap than reliable). The Beetle's ad campaign portrayed it as the antithesis of the large powerful cars being pushed by Detroit. As a result, the Beetle became a cultural touchstone for young people rebelling against everything their parents stood for—including large houses and equally large cars.

But among the decision makers at Volkswagen AG, the Beetle goes back much farther, to a darker time in German history. Arguably, the Beetle was the only good thing to come from Adolph Hitler's Third Reich. And while the Beetle played a significant role in the reconstruction of Germany after World War II, the Beetle itself represented basic transportation and nothing more. Unlike the American youth in the 1960s who fell in love with the Beetle, war-weary Germans in the 1950s may have bought Beetles to get around, but they aspired to newer, more sophisticated automobiles.

More importantly, the Beetle carried the stigma of owing its start to Hitler. While Hitler didn't invent the car, he was canny enough to exploit the popularity of a "people's car" for his own political ambitions. The idea of a cheap car for the working classes dovetailed nicely with earlier promises. Shortly after becoming Reich's Chancellor in 1933, Hitler promised at the opening of the

In the late 1960s, Volkswagen was exporting more than a half-million Beetles to the United States per year. *Volkswagen*

17

In the mid-1930s, Ferdinand Porsche's first prototype for a People's Car appeared. Porsche's early design evolved into this smaller, tidier V1 prototype, much closer to what became the original Beetle. *Volkswagen*

Berlin Motor Show to build Autobahns, reduce taxes on new cars, and generally encourage automobility. A year later at the same motor show, Hitler, who never drove but fancied himself as a car buff nonetheless, proposed his version of a people's car—the Volkswagen—after hearing that such a vehicle was already on the drawing boards of designers and engineers throughout Europe. (The Volkswagen didn't get its informal Beetle appellation until 1938 when one of the prototypes was so dubbed by the *New York Times*. In fact, throughout the history of the Beetle, the name never appeared on the car.)

One of those engineers was Dr. Ferdinand Porsche, an industry pioneer who designed a string of remarkable cars for companies like Daimler-Benz and Auto Union. In 1931, shortly after opening his own design office, he introduced Project 12 to his staff: a rear-engined, air-cooled car that someday would become the Beetle. According to Walter Henry Nelson, from his book *Small Wonder*, Porsche's car would be powered by a horizontally opposed, four-cylinder, air-cooled engine producing 26 horsepower. The motor would be mounted aft of the rear axle. The suspension would be a fully inde-

pendent setup using torsion bars that he invented. Instead of using conventional body-on-frame construction, Porsche's design called for unit-body construction. The body would be welded to a strong floorpan, and the engine and suspension would be mounted directly on the monocoque.

When Hitler called for his Volkswagen at the 1934 Berlin Motor Show, he said it should be a vehicle capable of 80 kilometers per hour that would consume no more than 4 to 5 liters of fuel per 100 kilometers and would cost less than 1,000 marks. Germany's auto industry was cool, if not indifferent, to the idea. These companies thought the cheapest small car that could be produced at a profit would cost 1,600 marks or more. The industry was content to build cars for the rich. Omnibuses, in their opinion, would handle the transportation needs of the working masses.

Faced with auto industry intransigence, Hitler commissioned Porsche to complete the design and study work, which was paid for by the German auto manufacturers' association. Though the group provided funding for the project, it showed little interest in the car's success.

Luckily for the automakers, progress at Porsche's shop, which was basically a garage at his home in Stuttgart, was slow. By the time he finished three prototypes and completed 30,000 miles of testing on each prototype, it was nearly 1938. The industry report on Porsche's efforts said the car needed more development.

The industry's foot-dragging convinced Hitler that he should nationalize the car effort. To fund the project, including the construction of a factory, he decided to tap the resources of the Nazi party-run labor union, the German Labor Front. The money would come from the Strength-Through-Joy (*Kraft-durch-Freude* or KdF) fund, which took 10 percent of all worker dues and earmarked it, some $120 to $200 million annually, for recreational purposes. Hitler

Following World War II, production slowly resumed at the bombed-out Wolfsburg factory under the direction of British occupation forces. This 1949 Beetle is ready for export. It features a split rear window, chrome bezels around the headlamps, chrome bumpers, and chrome wheel covers at the insistence of Heinz Nordhoff. *Volkswagen*

decreed that the Volkswagen would be known as the KdF-Wagen or Strength-Through-Joy car.

An unusual subscription plan was adopted where workers could put five marks a week away towards the purchase of a new Volkswagen. (By the end of World War II, more than 300,000 Germans had subscribed, generating some $67 million in payments. However, the Russians seized the money for war reparations.)

Along with a plant, a new city, KdF-Stadt (Strength-Through-Joy Town, later renamed Wolfsburg after the war), was built near the town of Fallersleben, midway between Hamburg and Berlin. But the plant was far from operational when Germany invaded Poland on September 1, 1939, to start World War II. The factory was converted to a patchwork complex that built military armaments, some airplane parts, 1.5 million stoves for use by troops on the Eastern Front, and, late in the war, components for V-1 rockets. Several Beetles were built as staff cars for the military, but mostly vehicle production consisted of Kubelwagens (forerunner

of the VW Thing) and an amphibious version of that car called the Schwimmwagen. The plant was heavily bombed in late 1944 and the town occupied by Americans in the spring of 1945.

Later, the plant was transferred to British authority and was reopened as a depot to repair and service military vehicles. Ironically, the facility was offered as war reparations to Henry Ford II. He declined, saying that this wreck of a factory and the car it produced had no value.

Two British officers proved crucial to Volkswagen's survival in the first days after the war. They were Colonel Charles Radclyffe, the man responsible for motor vehicles in the British zone of occupation, and Major Ivan Hirt, who Radclyffe had dispatched to the plant to oversee its operation.

Hirt recalled in his memoirs that those first years after the war were a time of great difficulty in finding raw materials to build cars and food to keep the line workers fed. At one point, a completed car was traded for a truckload of coal in order to keep the electric generators running.

While Hirt was able to keep the plant functioning, it was Radclyffe who ensured the future success of Volkswagen by hiring Heinrich "Heinz" Nordhoff. The former Opel executive had hoped to go back to work for the GM-owned automaker after the war but was told by American occupation forces that he would never work in the auto industry again. Nordhoff had managed Opel's Brandenburg truck factory, the largest and newest facility of its type in Europe at the time.

Production grew slowly, and by 1949, it reached 46,000. That year was also important for two events: the Cabriolet began production and two Beetles were exported to America through the Netherlands. Nordhoff decided that the export was the key to survival. Having worked for GM, Nordhoff had more than a passing familiarity with the U.S. market. He developed an export

19

The interior of the original Beetle was spartan. Instruments were limited to a speedometer and gas gauge. Nordhoff wanted export cars fitted with a cut-out panel in the center of the dash for a clock or a radio to meet the expectation of export markets. *Volkswagen*

model with door handles, chrome bumpers, wheel covers, and headlamp bezels. The car was painted in a high gloss paint and even had an opening in the dash for the installation of a clock or radio. In addition to sending cars to America, Nordhoff exported cars all over Europe.

As Europe began to rebuild and America's demand for cars continued to be insatiable during the postwar boom, Volkswagen's fortunes turned around quickly. By 1951, VW had turned a profit and two years later sold nearly 180,000 cars (about 40 percent to export markets). The plant was running at capacity, even though steel and other raw materials were still difficult to come by.

In 1957, U.S. sales of the Volkswagen Beetle had reached nearly 36,000 units when the company opened Volkswagen of America in Englewood Cliffs, New Jersey. Still, the image of the Volkswagen was not nearly what it would be in the 1960s. In the 1950s, the Beetle was still that funny little car. In 1959, Renault actually outsold Volkswagen 91,073 to 88,019, according to *Automotive News*.

Imports continued to grab a larger and larger share of the U.S. market and were finally being taken seriously by Detroit, which discovered the compact car. Even General Motors was working on its own response to the Beetle—a rear-engined, air-cooled car called the Corvair.

By 1960, little had changed on the Beetle since its debut. In 1952, the split rear window was dropped in favor of a small round one. It was later enlarged in 1958. Horsepower was increased slightly in 1961 from 36 to 40. And yet, the car's greatest successes still lie ahead of it. While Ferdinand Porsche's basic design had a timelessness to it, it was up to manufacturing and marketing men like Nordhoff and Carl Hahn, who headed Volkswagen of America, along with enterprising dealers to make the Beetle a cultural phenomenon.

Hahn, who was Nordhoff's personal assistant in Germany, took over as head of VW's U.S. division in January 1959 when he was only 32 years old. Hahn had a doctorate in political science from the University of Berne and had studied in France, Italy, and England. According to *VW—A History of an International Group*, Hahn decided that the company needed a unified corporate image right down to the design and look of its dealerships. "Above all, Hahn dedicated himself to establishing the public image of the Beetle as an appealing small underdog by means of fresh advertising campaigns. This decision was fueled by the ongoing compact car offensive taken by American automobile manufacturers."

The legendary agency that produced that campaign was actually discovered by one of VW's distributors. Arthur Stanton, who also served on the distributors' advertising committee, took out a single-page ad in the *New York Times* to announce the opening of Queensboro VW in New York. It was not unusual for a full-page dealer ad to appear in the *Times*, but what set it apart was the fact that it highlighted the dealership's service department and not new car sales.

The ad agency was Doyle Dane Bernbach. Hahn, seeing the ad and later talking to the agency, decided that DDB was the perfect fit for his goal of carving out a distinct public image for VW. From the uniform Howard Johnson's-like design of the dealerships (Hahn insisted on facilities that were as clean and uniform in appearance as the famous restaurant chain) to the simple clean ads that were honest and humorous in their approach, Volkswagen transcended the competition.

The ads in particular seemed almost anti-advertising, touting what would have been shortcomings, when compared to conventional automobiles, as virtues. One ad actually committed marketing heresy by not showing a car. The copy read: "We don't have anything to show you in our new models," which meant to say that the Volkswagen, unlike the competition, didn't indulge in annual styling changes just to make last year's cars obsolete.

As other import makes began to recede from the domestic market in the face of the onslaught of compact cars, Volkswagen sales climbed, thanks to the ad campaign, the upgraded dealer network, and above all, owner testimonials. Long before Saturn honed its image as a cult car, VW Beetle owners believed they were different and superior to others who merely bought what Detroit force-fed them.

Volkswagens also became associated with youth and the counterculture. Baby boomers bought the car as a statement against materialism. It was also inexpensive and relatively easy to work on. Lost in the reverie of youth, though, is the fact that the Beetle, as advanced as it was, had severe shortcomings, especially in colder climates. The air-cooled engine couldn't put out enough heat to keep the windows from frosting inside. The body

The quintessential VW Bug. Note the oval horn portals on the front—they inspired the air intakes on Concept 1. *Volkswagen*

rusted easily. The swing arm rear axle made for wicked handling. And the rear-engine design afforded little protection in head-on collisions.

As sales peaked at a half million units in the early 1970s, two pieces of legislation (the National Highway Safety Act of 1966 and the Clean Air Act of 1970) would soon make the Beetle obsolete. The car could not meet the crash requirements that were being phased in, and the air-cooled engine would be too difficult to certify for emissions. In 1979, Volkswagen sold its last Beetle in the United States. Assembly was eventually moved to Mexico where it remains in production for the Mexican market.

The last Beetle to be exported from Mexico to Germany made the trip in 1985. Six years later, J. Mays and Freeman Thomas met in Volkswagen's newest North American facility, a design studio about a 1,000 miles north of where the original Beetle was still being produced. The pair were plotting the birth of a New Beetle.

THREE

California Dreamin'

It all started over lunch in 1991. J. Mays, then head of Volkswagen's newly established California design center, was out with Peter Schreyer, a German designer on temporary assignment to the studio, and the two were commiserating over Volkswagen's lackluster performance in the U.S. market. "We concluded that when the name Volkswagen comes up, all people could talk about was the Beetle," Mays later recalled. "They didn't necessarily love the car for what it was; they loved what it stood for in their lives."

Returning from lunch, Mays called Freeman Thomas, his chief designer, into his office. Mays, an Oklahoman, and Thomas, a native Californian, had careers that tracked each other. While both had studied at the Art Center College of Design in Pasadena, California, their paths did not cross. Mays graduated in 1980, Thomas about a year later. Both worked in Germany, Mays for BMW and Thomas for Porsche. Later, Volkswagen separately recruited them. Mays went to Audi, while Thomas worked at Volkswagen before they teamed up at the new Simi Valley design studio.

"What do you think of doing a new Beetle?" Mays asked. It was a loaded question. The conversation with Schreyer helped Mays crystallize an idea he had while working on a recently completed concept car for Audi. That car was called the Avus, an aluminum-bodied 12-cylinder mid-engined supercar that recalled the Auto Union streamliners of the 1930s. The car would go on to be the smash hit of the 1991 Tokyo Motor Show; it was an important psychological boost for Audi to make a strong showing at a show where the Japanese automakers, ascendant throughout the 1980s, had always dazzled the public.

The Avus, which had a unique W-12 engine, polished aluminum bodywork, and a style that harkened back to the record-setting Auto Unions, was a bold statement. In one design, Mays and designer Martin Smith had created something that said Audi not only has a rich history, but is also on the cutting edge of technology. "It was the first time I made the connection that design is communication," Mays said. "It got me started on a different approach to design."

Early sketches of the New Beetle conveyed the humanity and whimsy of the original. *Volkswagen*

Freeman Thomas, a former designer for Porsche, quickly grasped J. Mays' vision for a new Beetle. *Volkswagen*

Mays wanted to do the same with the New Beetle. Freeman Thomas immediately grasped Mays' concept. "I loved the idea," Thomas said. As a car enthusiast, Thomas felt that making a connection with the original Beetle, via a new concept, would inject some spirit into a company that seemingly was going nowhere. Still, the idea was not a sure-fire winner.

"We had a chemistry in the studio of distinctly different personalities." Thomas continued, "We had a lot of people who didn't want to think anything about the past—all they wanted to do was push into the future, which we could respect as well. But we felt the future could also combine the equity of our past with the design geometry of the future."

While it's easy now to see the connection people make with the New Beetle, in 1991 it was difficult to imagine that the original Beetle was relevant in a world less than a decade away from the new millennium. In projecting concepts out to the end of the decade, there was a strong case to be made that Volkswagen should be expending its energy on breakthrough designs rather than past triumphs.

But both Mays and Thomas had given the idea of the New Beetle much more thought. It wasn't going to be retro just for the sake of being nostalgic, but rather it would be a reinterpretation of the original Beetle that would use, as a starting point, the classic elements and basic shapes that made it so popular to begin with.

"If you really study hard the Volkswagen geometry and Auto Union geometry, there's a common denominator," Thomas said. "The design engineer responsible for those cars was a man named Erwin Kamenda. We felt that was a very important ingredient because he had a way in which to put humanity into his design, almost a whimsy," Thomas explained. The Beetle's bug-like eyes, the round, friendly curves of the fenders, the running board-like rocker panels of the Bug were all elements that Kamenda penned. Kamenda had also worked on the Auto Union streamliners which Mays and Smith used as the inspiration for the Avus.

"So after that meeting," Thomas said, "we sat down and mapped out a plan. People have called us co-conspirators, and I think that's really a good phrase because that is kind of what we were. We were going against the grain and very few people would have agreed with us at that point. So we had to put together a strategy of how to sell the idea and how to fund the idea."

Mays was often quoted as saying the design took only three days—it was selling the project that took years.

Hartmut Warkuss, design director for the entire VW Group, encouraged Mays and Thomas to proceed with their designs for the New Beetle. Later, he would have to figure out how he was going to sell the idea to Ferdinand Piëch, the head of the Group. *Volkswagen*

Volkswagen's plummet in U.S. sales was both a blessing and a curse. A curse because money was tight. A blessing because the company knew it had to do something dramatic to turn its fortunes around in the largest car market in the world.

Mays and Thomas put together a project book with some rough sketches, ideas, and profiles and sent it to their boss at Volkswagen AG, Hartmut Warkuss. Warkuss liked what he saw and urged Mays and Thomas to continue to pursue the idea on the sly.

Warkuss didn't quite know how he was going to sell the idea to Ferdinand Piëch, who had taken over the Volkswagen Group that year. Warkuss had just moved into his job as design director for the entire group. As a result, both Warkuss and Piëch were busy getting used to their new jobs, and the idea went dormant for awhile. Thomas was sent to Audi in the summer of 1992 to work on a project. He continued to work on sketches in his hotel room in the evenings, and he'd talk to Mays about it on and off.

"The main thing was that we didn't want anyone to know about this idea because we didn't want the idea killed," Thomas said. In September 1992, Thomas returned to the Simi Valley studio, and he and Mays began to get serious. Warkuss was consulted, and he approved the idea to build two quarter-scale models.

In a small way, the state of California helped Mays and Thomas win that approval. At the time, California mandated that 2 percent of a manufacturer's total sales should be zero-emission vehicles (essentially electric cars) by the 1998 model year—although those standards have since been rolled back to 2002. The Simi Valley studio proposed that the Beetle be an electric vehicle study to meet that standard and dubbed the project "Lightning Bug."

"Calling it the Lightning Bug was more for us to get the car past first base," Thomas now admits.

At this time, Mays, Thomas, and designer Craig Durfey were working on sketches for a "new" Beetle. Mays and Thomas were creating designs that had separate fenders like the original, while Durfey took the approach of rounded integrated fenders that would give the look of the original Beetle but on a conventional car's body, Thomas explained. "Part of the iconistic elements were the side view, the arch of the roof, and the two arched fenders. We wanted the car to be distinctive from every single view. So we eliminated the third model, because it didn't stand out."

J. Mays wanted a car that captured the Volkswagen's sense of history and also that said the company was on the cutting edge of technology. Mays is now vice president of Design at Ford Motor. *Ford*

The concept behind the New Beetle's design is deceptively simple. From a side view, it is made up of three cylinders: the front fenders and wheels, a large central cylinder that is the passenger compartment, and the rear fenders and wheels. The front and rear views are almost identical—two round eyes and a smile created by the hood in the front and the hatch in the rear.

As simple and elegant as the design appears, getting there was another matter. "If you look back through the 1960s and 1970s, there have been attempts by design schools and design professionals to redesign the Beetle," Thomas said. "We can go back and see that everyone wanted to change it, to com-

J. Mays' work on the Audi Avus show car got him thinking about doing a new Beetle. *Volkswagen*

As the shape evolved, certain elements fell into place, like the front and rear cutlines that mimicked each other and made the car appear to be smiling. *Volkswagen*

pletely change it in the name of modernizing. What I feel we did differently was that we respected what was great about the original Beetle. We looked at the original shape and saw the benefits of that geometry. In other words, having the four separate fenders made it really easy for the user to repair or repaint if they got damaged. The arched roof—what kind of car has that kind of front headroom? When you look at the original Beetle from the side, it's actually kind of flat going through the top, but if you really interpret it as we did, it's an arch. That's what we wanted to do.

"We did from a design perspective what people do when you ask people about the old Beetle. They'll have nothing but great stories to tell you, but if they really were to go back into the 1950s and 1960s, they'll probably remember the cold winters when the glass froze up and the heater didn't give out enough heat and on and on and on," Thomas said. "The New Beetle is all about capturing all the warm fuzzy feelings and just giving you the good times."

In order to do that, the shape had to be friendly without being cartoonish. That's where the teaming of Mays and Thomas proved crucial.

"J. Mays' and my backgrounds are totally polarized," Thomas said. "[He], having been at Audi, worked at extreme geometric Bauhaus shapes. My background at Porsche, I did a lot of things that were emotional, whimsical types of

Further refinements secured the shape of the arc through the roof and the relationship of the fenders to the body. *Volkswagen*

Final sketches of the design that would become the New Beetle. The air intake is the single opening beneath the front bumper flanked by two driving lights. The side profile is comprised of three cylinders, two for the wheel arches and one large one that makes up the main cabin. *Volkswagen*

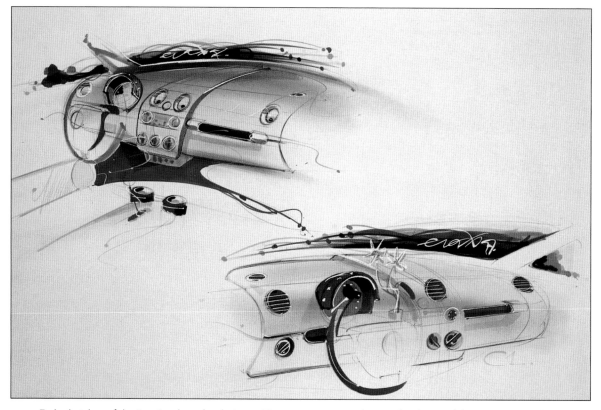

Early sketches of the interior show the designers' intent to carry over the circular theme of the exterior into the passenger cabin. The main instrument cluster is housed in a single round dial to mimic the original Beetle's layout. Many of the drawings already showed the bud vase. *Volkswagen*

shapes. From the beginning Jay went in a very strong geometric Bauhaus direction. I took a direction that was similar, but I warmed it up."

In the end, the two models actually came to be almost identical to each other. Mays and Thomas would look at each other's ideas and incorporate them on their own models.

Mays' model, for instance, had windows with sharp-edged corners, while Thomas's model used corners with a gentle radius. Mays' car had a flat front end, while Thomas' had a protruding nose to accommodate a bumper. Thomas developed the dual round intakes that mimicked the horn portals of the original as well as the way the A-pillar joins the front of the car.

The interiors of both cars were also very similar. Both carried over the circular themes from the exterior. There would be a single, round bezel behind the steering wheel to recall the old Beetle's basic instruments, which were a speedometer and a gas gauge. The interior would feature large body-colored panels and fascias, which copied the painted metal surfaces inside the original. Both designs had a grab handle on the dash and a bud vase.

"We wanted the front to be similar to the original Beetle in that there would be a hood section and two headlights like round eyes that created a smile," Thomas said. "We wanted the rear to mimic the front. We kept refining that

More circles. Two oval vents that flank a round analog clock dominate the center console. Even the controls on the radio and ventilation system are circles and dials. *Volkswagen*

and refining that on the two models to where we felt confident that we had the geometry to go to the full-size.

"After we finished these two scale models we photographed them. We actually took them to Malibu to shoot them in natural light," Thomas said. They tried to hide them as much as they could. But on a public beach it was impossible.

"We had a few passers-by, and they would say, 'What are those? Gosh they look like Beetles.' We'd say, 'Oh, we're just students, and we're just photographing our models.' They'd say, 'Oh, interesting,' and sort of move on."

By early 1993, they were ready to sell Warkuss on the idea of completing a full-scale model. But instead of bringing their boss into the studio to do the traditional walk-around, Mays and Thomas put together a presentation they would show first before even letting Warkuss into the studio. Ushered into a conference room, Warkuss was treated to a multimedia slide presentation using background music taken from the movie *Grand Canyon*. The presentation chronicled the rise and fall of Volkswagen in America, from selling just two in 1949 to the high point of a half-million in the early 1970s, back down to less than 50,000 in 1992.

Warkuss knew the depressing facts. But then, the music's tempo quickened, and the

The two quarter-scale models show Freeman Thomas' more emotional approach and J. Mays' Bauhaus influence. Thomas' design has rounded corners to the windows and a softer, more bulbous front end. Mays' design has sharp-angled windows and a flat face. *Volkswagen*

presentation began to show there was hope in the form of a reincarnated Beetle.

"We had to counteract many things in the German attitude towards cars and history with the American optimistic attitude of the '50s and '60s," Thomas explained. "We did this with music, and then we started showing slides of the New Beetle and the potential in the market and how it's just right. During the design process we came up with four words that reflected the Beetle philosophy—honest, simple, reliable, and original—and how that philosophy differentiated VW from the competition. That philosophy was more powerful for Volkswagen than almost anything else." Afterward, Warkuss rose and rapped his knuckles on the desk, which is the German equivalent of applauding madly. "This meeting was the turning point," Mays said. "It touched them. We knew then that the car is such an emotional fireball."

Warkuss was taken into the studio where he could examine the quarter-scale models and the preparations for the full-size study. He loved the concept and ordered the multi-media presentation to be shipped to Germany. By September 1993, Piëch had signed off on the project, now called Concept 1.

Rudiger Folten, who led the design team in Germany that transformed Concept 1 into the New Beetle, believes that the idea for the car could only have come from California. "The New Beetle proves how important our California studio is," he said. "Germany is distant from the Beetle. We have been making Golfs for over 20 years. The Beetle was part of history and nearly forgotten. In California the Beetle is still alive, and the designers there could see that."

"It has to be noted that this studio did not invent the Beetle," Thomas said. "We didn't invent the culture that went with it. We didn't invent all the Beetle stories. What Volkswagen did was identify with those stories, to be brave enough to present the car. There is a lot of intuitiveness with people involved with the car."

So sure were the designers that Concept 1 would become reality that the team tackled such production-oriented details as how the headlamps would function, where the mirrors would be positioned, and even the type of graphics that would be used on the instruments. "What we needed to do was create a foundation and give the tools for Volkswagen to actually build the car," Thomas said. "At this point, there was no discussion of a production car. We knew that if this thing would ever be shown to the public, it would be more difficult for Volkswagen not to build it than to build it."

Still, as excited as most of the designers were to be working on Concept 1, not everyone in the studio believed in the project. "We had a situation in the studio where some people wouldn't even come up and look at the car, they were so against doing this," Thomas said. "On the other side, we had people who couldn't get on the project fast enough. That is where the whole feeling of being a conspirator comes from. It's sort of like, we're not supposed to be doing this. I really applaud Hartmut Warkuss for standing behind us."

Even among those excited about the project, there was a fair amount of dissent on details like the bud vase. "We sketched up the idea, and I was amazed at how much controversy in the studio that caused," Thomas said. "I would say that maybe 30 percent of the people loved the idea and could deal with it, and 70 percent thought it was crazy. Why would we put a bud vase in a car? You have to realize that in every environment you have people that relate to certain periods of time with a lot of emotion and some people who don't." Thomas and Mays felt so strongly about the original Beetle and its bud vase that they felt the new car should have one. "In the end, we felt emotional enough about it," Thomas explained,

The Malibu photo shoot. Mays and Thomas take their quarter-scale models to a secluded beach north of Malibu to see what Concept 1 looks like in natural light. Mays' model, with its more angular lines, is yellow, while Thomas' rounder, more emotional design, is green. Note the vents at the back of both models, a detail that was later scrapped. Thomas' model has a see-through roof. Later, the models are photographed next to J. Mays' swimming pool, which gave off a color that inspired the green backlighting of Concept 1's instruments. *Volkswagen*

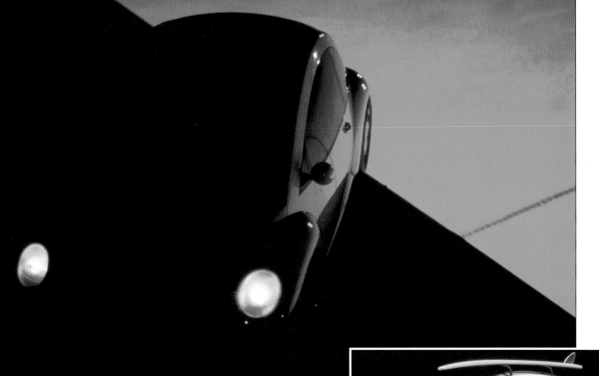

"that Jay and I said, 'We're going to put that thing in; we're going to have the vase in there.'"

Concept 1, contrary to popular belief, is not based on the Polo platform, the smallest car in Volkswagen's range. "When we did the quarter-scale models and began moving up to full-size, we blew the car up incrementally to where we felt really comfortable with the shape. We kept working with the interior packaging, and we brought it up to about 98 percent rather than 100 percent of the size we originally projected. When VW decided to start the production process, they researched all their platform groups, looking at which would be best to adapt. Originally it was Polo, but later it was decided that the Golf was a better fit. There's a bit of irony here—the original Beetle provided the basis for the Porsche 356. The New Beetle is going on the same platform as Audi's new TT, sort of a reinterpretation of the original 356.

"As for upsizing to the Golf, I'm pretty comfortable when I look at the car, drive it, and I'm inside it," Thomas said. "When you're developing the car, you're very critical about every millimeter of the size and shape. But it's different when you get out and you actually use the car and drive it and see it as a whole. When I drive this thing up to a Porsche dealer and it gets more of a crowd around it than the new Porsche 911, I say to myself, 'You know what? It's doing its job.' How can I criticize it?"

While there are few who can find fault now with the switch to the Golf platform, getting Concept 1 to that point had its share of critics. One critic in particular had the power to scuttle Mays' and Thomas' dream of a New Beetle.

Mays' original interior displayed a more angular geometric approach, while Thomas' was rounded and retro. Concept 1's final interior favored the Thomas design. *Volkswagen*

FOUR

Playing Around The Golf

In late summer 1995, VW chairman Ferdinand Piëch visited Volkswagen's test track at Ehra-Lessien not far from company headquarters to drive the New Beetle prototype. Development of the car had been conducted by an outside karosseriebauer, Volcke, located in Wolfsburg. After a turn at the wheel, Piëch was not a happy man. "Nobody liked it," Piëch recalled during a December 1997 interview in Wolfsburg. "I couldn't find even one person that said they liked the handling of this car."

Jens Neumann, board member in charge of North American sales, echoed Piëch's feelings. "We could find no enthusiasm for the qualities that the car needed to be a Volkswagen." The chairman of the board was prepared to kill the New Beetle. "For me, it was more dangerous that we never reach our target at the time. It was close to being canceled," Piëch said, with no hint of emotion.

Piëch, who came to the Volkswagen Group in 1991 after successfully turning around the Audi division, is the grandson of Ferdinand Porsche who designed the original Beetle. Piëch admits when he was nine, he was allowed to back a Beetle out from the family garage but bent the chrome bumper on a tree. In postwar Germany, it cost him a year's worth of pocket money to have the bumper hammered back into shape and re-chromed. His favorite vehicle of his grandfather's, however, was the four-wheel-drive Schwimmwagen, which helps explain why Piëch is credited with developing Audi into the all-wheel-drive powerhouse that it is today. So for Piëch, redoing the Beetle was problematical. As an engineer, he was anxious to prove himself in his own right. And yet, as one executive at Volkswagen AG put it, "It was a big test for him. To top a legend like the Beetle is a huge task for an engineer."

Freeman Thomas wanted a design so good that it would be more difficult for Volkswagen not to do the car. Conversely, Piëch and the engineers who drove the product development decisions felt that it wouldn't be right to make a car that was merely a design statement and not up to VW's standards for the rest of its product line. The Beetle prototype Piëch drove simply

Beauty shot of the New Beetle by Arni Katz. *Volkswagen*

Dr. Ferdinand Piëch, chairman of Volkswagen AG. Dr. Piëch is the grandson of the late Ferdinand Porsche, the original designer of the Volkswagen Beetle. *Volkswagen*

Polo, a vehicle not certified or sold in the United States, and yet the American market is where a new Beetle would have its strongest appeal. Part of the original plan for the new Beetle, which helped J. Mays and Freeman Thomas to initiate the project, was that it would be a test bed for alternative fuel or electric powertrains. Further complicating matters was the history. No one in Wolfsburg wanted to hear about the Beetle. For as beloved as the Bug was in America, it wasn't necessarily so in Europe.

There was one more hurdle, larger than all those factors combined. It was the Volkswagen Golf. The front-drive hatchback had become for Volkswagen today what the Beetle represented 30 years ago. Although Volkswagen of America sells only a handful of the hatchbacks in America, the parent company sells over 700,000 Golfs worldwide, representing roughly 20 percent of its total production. A major redesign of the Golf is a big deal. VW had just started the redesign of its biggest moneymaker for a 1998 launch when the Concept 1 was introduced in 1994 at the Detroit show.

So, when the Concept 1 was unveiled at the North American International Auto Show in

A clay modeler works on the New Beetle. Details such as the driving lights flanking the front air intake and the reflectors for the projector beam headlamps take shape. *Volkswagen*

didn't measure up. To Piëch, the right decision was to build a good car or none at all.

Such were the obstacles that lay in the path of Concept 1 becoming the New Beetle. Other companies, if handed a similar opportunity to build a car that would be such a smash hit on the show circuit, would have rushed it into production. But the factors behind the development of the New Beetle were so unique that getting it from the show stand to the showroom floor was hardly a foregone conclusion.

Keep in mind that the Concept 1 show car was about the size of VW's smallest car, the

The final design for the New Beetle. The round rearview mirrors of Concept 1 are replaced by rectangular ones. The rear bumper is more pronounced and a back-up light fills the left side opening that was the exhaust pipe on the show car. The exhaust now exits beneath the rear bumper. *Volkswagen*

Cutaway of the New Beetle. *Volkswagen*

Detroit in January 1994, Volkswagen showed a car developed by a bunch of Americans with an alternative fuel engine that didn't exist, built on a platform that couldn't be certified to U.S. standards. Furthermore, the guys making the decision on whether or not the car would be built were German executives who wanted no part of the past.

As a result of the sensation created by Concept 1, VW management finally gave the green light in November 1994. But the announcement was hardly a ringing endorsement. The three paragraph release read:

WOLFSBURG, Germany—Volkswagen's popular Concept 1 automobile, a design study car that created public and media sensation upon its unveiling at the 1994 North American International Auto Show in Detroit, Michigan, will be produced and on the market before the year 2000, Volkswagen confirmed.

The Volkswagen AG Board of Management gave its approval in November of 1994 for the development of Concept 1. The decision came in response to appeals from enthusiasts all over the world who embraced the design concept.

Volkswagen AG said the United States will be one of the main markets for the new car.

Since the business plan predicted that VW could sell only 100,000 New Beetles worldwide, with half the total going to the North American market, Wolfsburg was reluctant to devote the internal resources to develop the car when it had much work to do on a more important project, the Golf. "Everyone tried to prove that we

Cutaway of the Golf IV, which provides the underpinnings of the New Beetle. *Volkswagen*

could not do the Beetle in-house," Piëch later said. "It was a stepchild."

At this point, several critical decisions were made. Since it was Volkswagen of America that was lobbying so hard for the car, the Polo platform was abandoned. It was too small to meet U.S. safety standards.

"The reaction to Concept 1 convinced us that people wanted the old Beetle renewed," Piëch explained. "So we calculated what we thought we'd need to bring the Beetle to be best in class in crash, handling, brakes, and acceleration. The way we calculated it, it would have cost us what it takes to develop two cars to do it. We couldn't do it. At that point we had our styling department in California look at it as if one of our platforms could support a car that

continues the design philosophy of the old Beetle but rests on new systems. The Polo was too small, so the decision was made to go on the A-platform [the Golf]."

The larger Golf was already certified for the U.S. market, and by basing the Beetle on the A-platform, it could be built in the Puebla, Mexico, assembly plant that builds Golfs and Jettas (as well as the original Beetle for the Mexican market). VW could take advantage of the low-cost labor and the proximity to the United States to keep the sticker prices low and delivery to the New Beetle's largest market easy.

The change to the Golf platform meant the New Beetle would be much larger than Concept 1. The wheelbase grew from Concept 1's 92.1 inches to 98.9 inches. Overall length

VW's engineers focused on the launch of the all-new Golf, which forced the out-sourcing of the New Beetle's development. *Volkswagen*

increased to 161.1 inches, nearly a foot longer than Concept 1's overall length of 150.9 inches. Width grew from 65.1 to 67.9 inches, and the curb weight nearly doubled from 1,430 to 2,712 pounds. Industry analysts, catching wind of the change to the larger Golf platform, began to predict that if Volkswagen produced the car in limited numbers, it would cost more than the Golf, which was selling in the $15,000–$20,000 bracket. There was a gnawing feeling that a premium priced Beetle would be so unlike the original that it would limit its appeal. Suddenly, VW's projections of building 100,000 a year seemed optimistic to some observers.

While all these plans were coming together, other decisions were being made that nearly caused the project to unravel. The development of the Beetle lacked a crucial element to make it all work—ownership. As much as the marketing people in the United States wanted the car, they couldn't do the engineering necessary to develop it. That had to be done in Germany.

The decision to base the New Beetle on the Golf, while ultimately the Bug's salvation, almost killed the project. Engineers in Germany wanted to work on the new Golf. Few seemed interested in the New Beetle. So the development work was farmed out to Volcke and the American product planners. Their eyes firmly fixed on the bottom line, the planners insisted on changes to keep the sticker price low. Ultimately, those changes began to affect the development prototypes. While Concept 1 had been a marketer's dream, turning that vision into reality became an engineering nightmare.

"It really wasn't our car," Piëch said. "Some of the U.S. people wanted the cost down as much as possible, so it had drum brakes when

no A-class car [the Golf platform] in the whole group had drum brakes. The handling was bad. We wanted the Beetle to be as good as the Golf or better. It wasn't. So we had this big fight." Piëch was poised to cancel the New Beetle when Martin Winterkorn, the board member in charge of technical development, stepped in and insisted that the Beetle development be brought in-house.

"He [Winterkorn] convinced me to get rid of the external people and do it internally—not 100 percent internally—but on the key issues that give character to a car. Otherwise, the car's character would be of another personality," Piëch said. Winterkorn was convinced by Jens Neumann and design chief Hartmut Warkuss that the Beetle was crucial to turning around the company's image in the world's largest market.

Still, Piëch believed the Beetle had to be a real car or no car at all. Winterkorn assigned a small team, which was broken off from the Golf project, to finish the Beetle to Piëch's liking. It was decided that if the Beetle was going to be based on the Golf platform, it would be exactly like the Golf, from engines to chassis dynamics to equipment availability. "The platforms are the same," Piëch is fond of saying, "but each model wears a different hat." The Beetle would be a comfortable old homburg on the new Golf platform.

Slowly, more and more of the new Golf's components and structure were adapted to the Beetle. Rudiger Folten, a Beetle design team leader in Wolfsburg, liked the switch to the Golf platform. "It became a totally new car with a longer roof and hood and bigger bumpers. Concept 1 looks like a beautiful toy. The New Beetle looks like a car you can get into and drive. It feels right from the first moment."

Analysts weren't the only ones concerned about the use of the Golf platform. The media in Germany began to speculate that the Golf-based New Beetle would look nothing like Con-

Beneath the New Beetle Beats the Heart of a Golf

The Beetle shares all of the Golf's "hardpoints" (manufacturing lingo for where the fixtures are set to weld a structure together). The seats attach in the same place on the floor in the two cars, making the H-point—the position of the driver—almost the same, the only difference being that the Beetle driver sits a fraction of an inch higher due to a different thickness of the seat cushion. The 98.9-inch wheelbase is common, as are the front and rear overhangs. The only modifications to the basic Golf package include a new lower-profile radiator, a specific three-spoke steering wheel, and different air intakes and wiring harness.

The New Beetle initially offers the two engines found on the Golf in the United States: a 2.0-liter, four-cylinder gasoline engine and a 1.9-liter, turbocharged, four-cylinder diesel.

The 2.0-liter gas engine produces 115 horsepower at 5,200 rpm and 122 foot-pounds of torque at 2,600 rpm. The engine has a 3.25-inch bore and a 3.65-inch stroke with a compression ratio of 10:1. The front transversely-mounted engine has a cast-iron block and an aluminum cylinder head with a belt-driven single overhead cam and two valves per cylinder. The multi-port fuel-injected engine, which runs on regular unleaded gas, is water-cooled and is fitted with the latest in OBD II (On-Board Diagnostic) electronics and a three-way catalytic converter.

The 1.9-liter turbocharged, direct injection diesel produces 90 horsepower at 3,750 rpm and 149 foot-pounds of torque at 1,900 rpm. The cast-iron block has a 3.13-inch bore, and the stroke is 3.76 inches. The compression ratio is 19.5:1. Like the gas engine, it has a cast iron block and aluminum head, a single overhead belt-driven cam, and two valves per cylinder. The engine features the latest in direct injection diesel technology where the fuel, instead of being swirled in a pre-chamber, is injected and ignited directly in the cylinder head. The fuel is managed by an electronically controlled injection system that uses no mechanical inputs from the fuel pedal to fuel injection. VW says the engine is the equivalent of "drive by wire."

Like the Golf, the New Beetle is equipped with a choice of five-speed manual or four-speed automatic. The manual's gear ratios are identical through the first three gears, while the diesel's drops into a 0.97 overdrive in fourth compared to the gas engine's 1.03 ratio. Fifth is 0.84 for the gas and 0.76 for the diesel. Final drive is also different: the gas engines have a 4.24 gear, while the diesel is equipped with a 3.39 final drive. On the automatic, gasoline versions have a shorter second gear (1.55 versus 1.44); third is 1:1 on both, and the gasoline version has a taller overdrive at 0.68 to the diesel's 0.74. Final drive on the gas automatic is 4.88 and 3.71 on the diesel.

The new Golf's steering and independent suspension was carried over intact to the Beetle. The power-assisted rack-and-pinion steering has a 17.8:1 ratio and takes 2.5 turns of the steering wheel to go lock-to-lock. It allows the Beetle to have a turning circle of 35.4 feet. The front suspension is a MacPherson strut design with lower wishbones, stabilizer bar, and coil spring struts. The rear suspension employs a "V" profile independent torsion beam axle with integral sway bar and trailing arms. The torsion beam axle is mounted to the vehicle with Volkswagen's unique track-correcting bushings, which help keep the rear end in check during spirited driving.

The New Beetle also benefits from a revision in the new Golf's rear suspension. The coil springs have been separated from the shocks and relocated below the longitudinal suspension members. This eliminates the need for suspension strut towers that would take up extra room in the trunk.

The basic structure of the Beetle is galvanized sheet steel, which allows VW to offer a 12-year warranty against corrosion or rust perforation. Laser welding techniques developed for the Golf enable the Beetle to share the same narrow panel gap tolerances and high torsional rigidity of the body. The only other difference from the Golf in body construction, aside from the shape, is that the Beetle uses plastic front fenders that are bolted to the unit body. That shape also contributes to a much higher drag coefficient—the Beetle clocks in at 0.38 Cd compared to the Golf's 0.31. But is the shape, in the eyes of the buyer, that makes all the difference between a good car and a great one.

cept 1. One of Germany's leading car magazines, *Auto Motor und Sport*, ran artists' drawings of some truly ugly Bugs. As a result, a show car with Golf dimensions was prepared for the 1995 Tokyo Motor Show in order to put that speculation to rest. Still, the design of the car was not final. Folten said the data control model, upon which the production cars are based, was not released until late November 1995, about a month after the Tokyo show.

The swimming pool green lighting of Concept 1's instruments changed to incandescent blue. *Volkswagen*

Detail changes between Concept 1 and the New Beetle are easily picked out. The twin air intakes on the nose are gone, replaced by a bumper that protrudes beneath the plastic front fascia. A single large air intake is cut out beneath the front bumper. Folten said other touches, like vents beneath the rear window to mimic the air intakes on the original, have been dropped along with the radius-shaped corners on the windows. "We had to decide if we were going to make a nostalgic Beetle it should be a car that is a new design," Folten said. "If you get too near the original [in design], it's not serious. It becomes a joke on wheels. This is a new car, and it looks fresh."

Folten is particularly proud of the interior, which the German design staff made over. The Concept 1 interior was stark, with greater use of body-colored fascias to recall the exposed painted metal surfaces found in the original. "The dashboard is totally new," Folten said. "While we retained the spirit of Concept 1, the overall appearance and functions are geared more towards the consumer." The basic shapes are the same, including the single large dial that incorporates the speedometer, tachometer, and fuel gauge, as well as the dash-mounted grab handle, but the rest of the surfaces are covered in a textured matte finish. The modules are more sculpted, warmer looking, and user friendly. The only body-colored trim pieces are on the door. Even the bud vase was moved from the right of the center console to the left. The goal was to make an interior that a customer could live with on a day-to-day basis rather than show off as a far-out design. Some of the elements of this new design are being used on other VW products like the recently launched Lupo, a replacement for the Polo in Europe.

Freeman Thomas observed, "The interior is better than the show car interior. That has to do with further development including looking at textures. The new texture on the dashboard, the kind of gridded texture they used, is just fantastic."

Four months later, at the Geneva show, Folten's group was ready to show off the final shape and finished interior of the New Beetle. That car was equipped with two features not yet available on production New Beetles: VW's syncro four-wheel drive and a huge sliding glass roof developed by Porsche. By now, the New Beetle was well on its way to production trim, where it would use 80 percent of the Golf's underskin components. Again, these extra touches further fueled speculation among industry observers that Volkswagen would have to price the Beetle somewhere between $18,000 and $22,000. Even though the car continued to be warmly received, pricing began to loom as a major factor among auto analysts on whether or not the Beetle would succeed.

The final battle fought between the product planners, interested in keeping the cost in line, and

Reports that the New Beetle would be Golf-based fueled speculation that it would look nothing like Concept 1. In response, VW unveiled a Golf-based New Beetle concept at the 1995 Tokyo Motor Show. Some details, like the opaque headlamps and the chrome tab beneath the VW logo on the rear, were changed on the production car. *Volkswagen*

the engineers, insisting that the Beetle handle just like the Golf, was over the brakes. In Piëch's mind, the drum brakes had to go. In the United States, the prototypes being used in the ad shoots and the cars running up durability miles that were being snapped by spy photographers all had drum brakes. In August 1997, Piëch got his wish. Four months before the production car would make its worldwide debut, at the same auto show that gave Concept 1 to the world four years earlier, the decision was made to go with four-wheel disc brakes. The upgrade employs 11-inch vented rotors in front and 9.4-inch solid discs in the rear. The mechanical package was in place; the only thing left was the price. The New Beetle was ready to roll.

Ferdinand Piëch would go to Detroit a happy man.

The final production version of the New Beetle was shown at the 1996 Geneva Motor Show. The car was displayed with the 1.9-liter TDI diesel. The only piece of body-colored trim left from Concept 1 is the windowsill on the door panel. Although the car looks ready for production, some of the details and options that appear on the car had yet to go into production. They include the two-tone seats, Syncro all-wheel drive, and the large sunroof. *Volkswagen*

FIVE

Hug It or Drive It?

Fun. That's what the Beetle is all about. Freeman Thomas put it best when he said, "Imagine there was no original Beetle and we did this car. People would think we were crazy."

But once upon a time there was a Beetle, which makes VW crazy like a fox. Trading on the goodwill of a car it hasn't sold in the United States in 20 years, Volkswagen has garnered more good publicity with the New Beetle introduction than any slick commercial strategically placed during the Super Bowl.

On January 5, 1998, four years to the day from the unveiling of Concept 1, Volkswagen prepared to launch the New Beetle with the kind of hype worthy of the Super Bowl. Using nearly 30,000 square feet of Detroit's Cobo Hall, VW constructed a multi-level stand that featured VW's current lineup of cars, the Golf, Jetta, and Passat on the main floor and an area twice as large on the lower level just for the New Beetle. Called "New Beetle World," this separate display showed off six New Beetles including one autographed by randomly selected showgoers, which was destined for the VW Museum in Wolfsburg. During the show, the wait for the escalators to take visitors to New Beetle World was as long as 50 minutes.

VW chairman Ferdinand Piëch had reasons to smile other than the New Beetle launch. As he stood before 2,500 journalists and was broadcast live on a worldwide satellite feed, he detailed VW's worldwide results, which included 4.3 million sales in 1997, an increase of 7.4 percent. VW was the fifth largest carmaker and No. 1 in Europe for the 13th consecutive year.

The New Beetle, though exciting to Americans, was actually just a small part of Piëch's overall ambitions for VW. He took the opportunity to announce plans for the company's global lineup to grow from 41 to 51 models by the end of the decade. And it seemed by his remarks that he was still perplexed by the incredibly positive response to the Concept 1 and the New Beetle. "Four years ago, VW presented the Concept 1 design here in Detroit," Piëch said. "At that time, we certainly did not expect such a favorable reaction from the public, our dealers, and the press. We were overwhelmed. From the very first moment, it seemed we were almost forced by the customer's voice to make a real car out of the concept."

Hug it or drive it? *Joe Wilssens*

Dr. Jens Neumann, the head of Volkswagen's North American sales, originally guarded his enthusiasm for the New Beetle, but when it was finally unveiled in Detroit, he could barely contain his excitement for the car. *Volkswagen*

Piëch said that the larger Golf-based Beetle "has grown up and fits the American market. The New Beetle cannot deny its origins and the originality of its shape. I am very proud to present the New Beetle in the United States. It was here that this Volkswagen was affectionately called the Beetle, a name that quickly spread all over the world. We believe the Beetle is not just another car. It will stand out on North American roads." But Piëch's real feelings about the New Beetle and its role in VW's universe was summed up in one line: "Despite all the high expectations we have for the New Beetle, one thing is for sure. Volkswagen will never be again the one-car car company."

While Piëch correctly grasped the big picture of VW as a global player, Jens Neumann, the Volkswagen AG board member in charge of North American sales and marketing, seized upon the significance of the New Beetle's launch in the United States. The company's fortunes had plummeted from a half-million sales in the early 1970s to less than 50,000 by 1993. Volkswagen had all but disappeared from the U.S. market. All the ad money in the world couldn't get people to talk about, much less buy, the company's current product in a marketplace glutted with sedans just like VW's.

Of all the board members, Neumann was the one German executive who keenly understood the American love affair with the Beetle. Trained as a lawyer in Geneva, Switzerland, Neumann completed high school in Baltimore, Maryland, as an exchange student. In fact, a 1961 photo of Neumann, wearing a football uniform and sitting on the hood of a Bug, was shown to a VW's dealer convention where he was the featured speaker.

Reporters scrambled for the 10,000 press kits VW distributed after Dr. Ferdinand Piëch unveiled the New Beetle at the Detroit Auto Show in front of an audience of 2,500 journalists and a worldwide television feed. *Volkswagen*

The media wasted no time in scrutinizing the cars at the Detroit Auto Show. A particularly popular model of the New Beetle with heat sensitive paint invited onlookers to press the flesh to make different designs appear. *Volkswagen*

The lower level of Detroit's Cobo Hall was converted into New Beetle World, a space that quickly became jammed with people. *Volkswagen*

Unlike the reserved Piëch, Neumann bounded to the stage and could barely contain his enthusiasm. "It's a great day in Detroit," Neumann beamed. "We now have the honor to present to you something which we would all agree is very exciting: the birth of a legend, a love affair continued, a dream come true. During these past four years, we have received thousands of letters and phone calls from all around the world. People offering ideas, sharing personal stories, and asking us again and again, 'Are you really bringing the Beetle back?' The answer is 'nope.' We're not bringing the Beetle back. We bring you the New Beetle—a very modern car that we all seem to have known for some time—an evolutionary work of art that has become dear to our hearts long before we could touch it for the very first time.

"Yes, it is Volkswagen's most advanced technology, a car for the twenty-first century," Neumann continued. "It handles great; it has all the safety features; it is built to the highest quality standards. All of this is understood and appreciated. But that's not why people will want to buy the New Beetle. They will want this car to make them feel good about themselves, to share a smile with others. To have fun together. The New

Beetle is an inspiration to live, or you could say the New Beetle is optimism on wheels."

Still, there was the question of price. Analysts felt that if the New Beetle was priced above $20,000 it would make it unaffordable to young people and make nostalgic baby boomers think twice about plunking down money on hazy memories. Neumann recognized this, saying, "Of course, this dream with a sound system is not for free, but we think it's not expensive either." You could hear a pin drop as he paused to announce the price. "The base price will be 19,940 [pause] Canadian dollars or 15,200 U.S. dollars."

The car was the hit of the show. The 10,000 press kits, each with a replica of the New Beetle's bud vase, were distributed to mobs of reporters. At the black-tie charity preview on the night before the show's opening, the escalators had to be stopped in order to handle the crush of people trying to get to the Cobo Hall basement to catch a glimpse of the car. Meanwhile, the show stands at the opposite end of the hall were as deserted as a ghost town.

The reaction was foreshadowed in marketing clinics. Neumann said the response to the New Beetle was amazing. "People of all nationalities, all ages, divergent life experiences, different incomes, and different religions all behaved the same when they first saw the car: They smiled; they walked deliberately toward the car; they gently touched the roof or the fender and followed the curve of the sheet metal. If the car were a person, they'd hug it, shake hands, or put their arm around it. There's a delightful, approachable familiarity about this car. When people are in the car, they feel good, at ease. It's like making a friend at first sight."

Driving the New Beetle

Once you're behind the wheel, out on the open road, you see smiles on the faces of just about everyone who encounters the New Beetle. There's a glimmer of recognition, quickly followed

The New Beetle at speed. *Volkswagen*

by broad, toothy grins. Of course, the requisite arm-waving and pointing accompany the smiles. Beetlemania is infectious. Looking in the rearview mirror, you can see your own smile.

Better still is the fact that the New Beetle, by utilizing the same underpinnings as Volkswagen's all-new Golf, is a car that can bring a smile to any enthusiast's face. The fact that VW chairman Ferdinand Piëch insisted upon it comes through. The New Beetle drives just like the Golf. The car, as Piëch decreed, is just wearing a different hat.

And what a hat! The body definitely recalls the Beetle, but at the same time, it's completely modern. The most noticeable change from tra-

dition is that the New Beetle is a hatchback. But the rounded shape, the distinct fenders, single head and tail lamps, and a face that looks like it's smiling is all Beetle.

Unlike the original, the curves and lines conceal a thoroughly modern automobile. Take the single flush round headlamps, for instance. They actually house multiple lamps including projector beam headlights, turn signals, and daytime running lights. Though the front fascia and fenders look like a single piece, they are actually two plastic pieces bolted to the steel body. Access to the rear hatch is hidden beneath the large VW badge on the back. Slide it sideways, and a neat little chrome pull pops out. Pop the hatch, and you have 12 cubic feet of stowage plus a full-size spare mounted beneath the floor of the cargo area.

Even more differences lurk beneath the slick-styled shell. The New Beetle is the complete opposite of the original. It is front- versus rear-wheel drive, liquid- versus air-cooled, inline four versus boxer four. It is also larger than the original, riding on a 98.9-inch wheelbase. The New Beetle is 67.9 inches wide, 161.1 inches long, and 59.5 inches high. Inside, 96.3 cubic feet of total interior volume can be found. For perspective, consider that a 1967 Beetle 1500 rode on a 94.5-inch wheelbase, measured 160.6 inches overall, and weighed in at 1,790 pounds, more than half a ton lighter!

And unlike the original, the New Beetle has a wide range of standard equipment unheard of in the original including CFC-free air conditioning, a micron air filtration system, front and side airbags, four-wheel disc brakes, power rack-and-pinion steering, tinted glass, anti-theft alarm, power door locks, and an AM/FM stereo with cassette. The option list is relatively short: CD player, cruise control, leather interior, heated front seats, leather wrapped steering wheel and shift knob, power windows, and a power glass sunroof.

Inside, the New Beetle has virtually the same seating position as the Golf. The relative height of the vehicle makes sliding in behind the wheel an easy task. Once settled in the front buckets, the seating position is very familiar. It's not at all like the original Beetle, with its thinly padded seats, flat dash, thin steering wheel, and in-your-face windshield. Rather, the feel behind the steering wheel is remarkably Golf-like. You sit upright. The shift lever is within easy reach, positioned just off your right thigh.

But the interior styling has a character all its own. It's decidedly Beetle retro. The instrument cluster resembles the single speedometer of the original, though in the lower quadrants of the face are a tachometer and gas gauge. At night, the instruments are backlit with an incandescent blue. You can't help but notice the bud vase, nestled right there between the steering wheel and the radio controls. The switches and the dials for the heating and air conditioning system are large and simple to use. Logically, at least for channel surfers, the radio is mounted high in the dash and below it is the HVAC system with clearly marked positions for heat, air conditioning, and venting. The adjustable steering wheel, which has the same beneath-the-column handle as the Passat and Audi A4, is within easy grasp. The padded, three-spoke wheel moves up and down and telescopes.

The New Beetle can be outfitted in a choice of three materials (vinyl, cloth, or leather) and three trim colors (beige, gray, and black). The windowsills are plastic pieces color-keyed to the exterior. While black and red fairly match the outside color, the matte finish of the plastic on the yellow cars picks up a green from the standard tinted windows and comes across as a funkier yellow than the exterior paint.

The dashboard is mounted in the same place as the Golf's, but with the different body shape, the interior comes across as being cab forward without the benefits of the extra room. You have the large A-pillars that arc out in front of you and hamper forward three-quarter vision. The deep dash shelf reflects slightly into the glass.

The front seats, which adjust up and down with a ratcheting lever, pop up and forward to ease access to the fold-down rear seats. Rear cabin space, however, is limited. Sitting there for long periods of time is difficult. A 5-foot, 9-inch frame means your head is snug against the top of the rear window. Anyone larger has to slouch. The New Beetle is more of a two-plus-two than a four-passenger vehicle. But because of the unique shape, the front passengers enjoy an abundance of headroom, and the snug buckets offer good lateral support.

At launch, engine choices were limited to a choice of the 90-horsepower, 1.9-liter turbo-diesel (which pushes the entry-level base price up from $15,200 to $16,475) or the 115-horsepower, 2.0-liter, four-cylinder gasoline version. For the 1999 model year, a 150-horsepower, 1.8-liter, turbocharged inline four with five valves per cylinder will be offered.

Twist the key (it's located on the column like the Golf, which is strange since many cars have returned to dash-mounted locks like the original Beetle), and the engine kicks over with the familiar muted tones of current Volkswagens. In retrospect, that's perhaps the biggest disappointment with the new car—it looks like a Beetle, but it certainly doesn't sound like one. Run with a group of vintage Beetles, and you'll be reminded how wonderful and satisfying the air-cooled thump-thump-thump of the original can be.

Still, the base eight-valve, 2.0-liter gas engine promises better levels of performance than the original, though the 0–60 acceleration of 10.6 seconds as recorded by *Road & Track* is not beneath the 10-second level that most cars are capable of today. When equipped with a five-speed manual, the engine does show off some flexibility. Spooling the engine up to just over 2,000 rpm allows you to put the peak torque of 122 foot-pounds to good use. The diesel, though much stouter with 149 foot-pounds of torque at only 1,900 rpm, launches strongly but quickly runs out of steam. VW reports a 0–60-miles-per-hour gait of 13 seconds with a manual. Automatic-equipped turbo-diesels will certainly have acceleration that is best described as leisurely. The New Beetle in either form will have exceptional range. The 14.5-gallon fuel tank will allow the

RIGHT AND NEXT SIX PAGES
A New Beetle photo gallery. *Arni Katz, Volkswagen*

turbo diesel to go over 600 miles at its most efficient 48 miles per gallon highway rating, while the 2.0-liter gas should go nearly 450 miles at 31 miles per gallon highway.

The five-speed short throw manual is easily and precisely moved up through the gears. The whole drivetrain comes across as competent and workmanlike, which is just fine for someone who wants to get around in style but isn't necessarily interested in winning a stoplight grand prix. Clutch take-up is light and progressive, which matches the crisp throttle response. The New Beetle has all the visceral responses we've come to expect from Volkswagens: a little busyness from the engine and controls that feel as if they are directly connected to the things they work. If you like the way Golfs and Jettas drive, you'll love the New Beetle. Structurally, it is solid with good noise, vibration, and harshness damping. Some tire, wind, and drivetrain noises penetrate the cabin.

The ride is well-damped and comfortable thanks to the straightforward suspension. MacPherson struts with lower transverse arms and coil springs are located up front, and an independent twist beam axle with coil springs and shocks suspend the rear of the car. The front and rear anti-roll bars help provide relatively flat cornering.

The New Beetle is quite neutral for a front-driver. There's a slight bit of understeer dialed in, and when pushing in corners, you can make the line tighten slightly by letting off the gas. Basically, the suspension offers up no big surprises and is very forgiving to the over-enthusiastic.

Also acting as a safety net for the exuberant are the 11-inch front and 9-inch rear disc brakes (vented front, solid rear). They haul the car down quickly from 60 miles per hour. *Road & Track* measured 155 feet with little fade. Four-wheel ABS is offered as an extra cost option.

The power-assisted rack-and-pinion steering is quite accurate, though a little heavy at

lower speeds. It takes a bit of effort to move it off center at speed. Still, for those who like the muscular feel of German steering, it is most satisfying. The steering communicates directly at speed and feels as taut as the suspension. Unlike the Golf which rides on standard 14-inch wheels and tires, the New Beetle fills up its wheel arches with 16-inch steel wheels fitted with 205/55R16H all-season radials. Six-spoke alloy wheels are optional.

The performance level of the New Beetle, though, is only half the story. Words can't describe the reaction that comes from driving a car that became a cultural icon (largely on the strength of the car that preceded it) even before it went on sale to the public. The New Beetle stands out in a sea of small cars that look like they've come from the same aerodynamic cookie cutter or were drawn from the template of the BMW 3 Series.

More than just being different, the New Beetle evokes such a strong emotional response from those who encounter it that you have to be prepared to become an extrovert if you own one. Strangers will talk to you. Kids will desert playgrounds just to see and touch the car. For now, it will be like owning one of the first Dodge Vipers, except that you'll have some $35,000 extra in your pocket. Starting at $15,200, most New Beetles will probably list out in the $17,000–$18,000 price range with extras like a CD player and sunroof.

Someday the latest Beetlemania, like most fads, will fade. The smiles will be replaced by mere grins. Still, you'll be able to console yourself that beneath this familiar shape beats the heart of a real car. And that's no small consolation.

RIGHT AND NEXT TWO PAGES
Ehra-Lessien photo shoot of the New Beetle, including engine detail shot, door panel, and hatch. *Volkswagen*

SIX

The New Beetlemania

"The New Beetle will reinforce the emotional link to our customers and friends. This emotion will appeal to both men and women, both young and young-at-heart. This car is for people who see the world's glass as half full. It's original, honest, and timely. It truly represents the core values of Volkswagen. Its values transcend classes and social status . . . "
Jens Neumann, New Beetle introduction, North American International Auto Show, January 5, 1998

The New Beetle is a sensation. It's not just a new car, it's a cultural phenomenon. Tickle Me Elmo on wheels. Motorized Beanie Babies. Rolling Viagra. Evidence of the global appeal of the car comes from Volkswagen going to the extraordinary length of reminding dealers that their franchise agreements specifically prohibit them from exporting cars and discouraging them from charging more than the sticker price. More cars appeared on car broker lots than in VW dealerships as dealers quietly slipped cars to auction or owners sold them for a small profit within the first few weeks of taking delivery.

Reports of cars going for as much as $4,000 over sticker were not uncommon. Still, the New Beetle was such a good news story that reports of over-sticker pricing and speculation failed to use the term "gouging." Instead, in the frenzy to own a New Beetle, the cars were being "scalped" like they were tickets to a hot concert.

The New Beetle has also had its intended effect on overall VW sales, which jumped 50 percent in the months following the car's launch. People were not just snapping up New Beetles, but Passats, Jettas, and Golfs as well.

The New Beetle has been featured on magazine covers, the front page of *USA Today*, CNN, and a host of other broadcast and print media. A Los Angeles radio station, KROQ, sponsored a contest called "Live in it and win it" where the last of four contestants to live in a New Beetle over a two-week period would win the car. "The problem was, none of them fell out of the contest," said Jeff LaPlant, general sales manager for Volkswagen of Santa Monica, which supplied the car. "They all stayed in the

A car conceived, built and promoted on the basis of a 30 year-old cultural icon? That is exactly the gamble Volkswagen was willing to take on the New Beetle. *Jim Frenak*

ABOVE AND OPPOSITE
The New Beetle earns high marks from the Insurance Institute for Highway Safety in offset crash tests. Notice how the cabin remains virtually intact. *IIHS*

same car. They slept in it. They ate in it. They were only allowed out for bathroom breaks." The contest could be viewed live on the Internet, and the site logged more than 12 million hits. When it became apparent that no one was dropping out, at the urging of KROQ, LaPlant scrambled to find three more cars so all four could end up owning a New Beetle.

To Freeman Thomas and J. Mays, the excitement surrounding the launch of the New Beetle validated their intuition. To Volkswagen of America, it put them back in the North American market where the brand had all but disappeared. To Ferdinand Piëch and Volkswagen AG, it was important, but so was the decision to buy Rolls-Royce.

Will the New Beetle's celebrity status last? Crucial to that point is not how long the New Beetle remains the darling of those who push the levers of pop culture, but rather how well it

The New Beetle suffers only $134 in rear bumper damage in a low-speed impact with a post. *IIHS*

Original Beetles are still being produced in Mexico on a line adjacent to New Beetle assembly. The older cars are virtually hand-built. *Volkswagen*

functions as a real car, a car that just happens to have a lot of personality. As production ramps up in Puebla, Mexico, and Volkswagen hits its goal of selling 50,000 to 60,000 New Beetles a year in the United States, the dealer markups will eventually disappear, as they have in the past with the Mazda Miata and Dodge Viper.

The ultimate success of the New Beetle hinges on how it is marketed, its safety and quality, and whether or not Volkswagen continues to evolve and improve the car. Like the marketing campaign for the original Beetle, advertising will play a critical role in fixing the New Beetle in the consciousness of the American public. Neumann's marketing philosophy is simple, one that grew largely from the clinics that showed people are already predisposed to liking the New Beetle.

"We've decided to simply show the car, show its shape, and get out of the way," he explained. "We don't try to describe it. We don't explain the features. We don't spoil individual dreams and memories by talking about the hardware. We get out of the way and let people define this car in quite personal terms. We let them establish their own personal relationship and let them want to drive the car. So the new advertising is consistent with our 'Drivers Wanted' campaign. It is an invitation in the Volkswagen spirit of 'That is what we are about. Is that what you are about?' Our campaign is 'Volkswagen—the company that loves people.'"

The campaign, put together by Boston-based Arnold Communications, has the look and feel of the legendary Doyle Dane Bernbach campaign that put VW on the map in the United States. There are no spokespeople.

The car is the star. The copy is simple, just one or two lines. Where the DDB ads had several paragraphs, the New Beetle campaign suffices with just a few lines that gently poke fun at the original Beetle. One sample line is: "Comes with wonderful new features. Like heat." Another even admits the New Beetle is no rip-snorting performance car. It says: "0–60? Yes." Another plays off the emotional appeal of the car by asking, "Hug it? Drive it? Hug it? Drive it?"

tute of Highway Safety released results for its 40-mile-per-hour offset crash test of the New Beetle that showed the car scoring best out of the 16 small cars tested by the group.

That's quite a feat for the spiritual successor of a car that no less than Ralph Nader roundly criticized in 1966. Back then, he told Congress, "It is hard to find a more dangerous car." Those hearings resulted in the stringent safety laws that the original Beetle could no longer meet by the late 1970s. But now, according to the IIHS, "The reincarnated Beetle's crash-worthiness is as up-to-the-minute as its styling is retro."

The IIHS determined that the New Beetle was the only model to earn an overall evaluation of "good" and a "best pick" designation. It also earned high marks for structure performance in the Institute's front offset crash test. The large arc of the A-pillars helped stiffen the body structure so well that the New Beetle outperforms the new Golf in offset crash tests. In fact, after the Golf performed poorly in similar offset crash tests in Germany, Ferdinand Piëch ordered production stopped until additional pieces could be welded to that car's A-pillars to further strengthen the safety cage.

Other features that the IIHS found noteworthy on the New Beetle included good geometry on the head restraint placement, which helps minimize whiplash; strong bumpers that afforded the best protection in low speed impacts (under the IIHS test, the Beetle suffered only $134 worth of damage); and the use of both safety belt pretensioners and side airbags.

Of the 40-mile-per-hour test (which is 10 miles per hour faster than the full-frontal impact requirement for U.S. certification), the IIHS' Brian O'Neill said, "The structural performance was impressive. The front-end crush zone managed the crash energy very well so that damage was kept away from the occupant compartment. The driver space was maintained so well

These clever ads may draw lookers to the showroom, but if the New Beetle is shoddily built or lacks the qualities of a real car in the areas of safety and performance, people will quickly see the retro styling as a gimmick. That's why Piëch's insistence that the New Beetle be a real car, with such features as front and side airbags, is crucial to the car's future. His insistence on technical competence paid off much earlier than anyone within Volkswagen ever dreamed. On May 4, 1998, the Insurance Insti-

The New Beetles are made on a new line at the Puebla factory. Many of the components are pre-assembled modules which reduces the man-hours needed to produce each car. Only 2,000 of the plant's 15,000 workers build the New Beetle. Puebla will produce over 120,000 of the cars in the first full year of production. *Volkswagen*

that, after the 40-mile-per-hour crash tests, the deployed airbags were the only obvious indications inside the occupant compartment that the impacts had been serious. Later, when we measured the precise amounts and pattern of the intrusion into the New Beetle's occupant compartment, our initial assessment was confirmed. There was much less intrusion than in the other small cars we previously tested."

While getting quick feedback on the safety issue will only help bolster the New Beetle's reputation, overall vehicle quality will take much longer to establish. Worldwide production of the New Beetle is based in Volkswagen's sprawling Puebla, Mexico, assembly plant about 60 miles southeast of Mexico City. Not only is Puebla home for the New Beetle, it is also responsible for producing the original Beetle on an assembly line next door to where the new car is built. In 1997, VW built over 30,000 of the originals for the Mexican market. Puebla also builds all Jettas (about 100,000) and Golfs (less than 30,000) for the U.S. market. With the introduction of the New Beetle and an all-new Jetta on the way, the redesigned Golf will no longer be built in Mexico, and the U.S. market will be supplied from Wolfsburg.

The Mexican plant, however, has had a reputation for difficult labor relations and spotty quality. When Ferdinand Piëch took over the Volkswagen Group in 1991, one of his first priorities was to improve worker relations at the plant and fix the quality problems. In its first 25 years of operation, the plant, which was built in 1966, had three different unions organized and

disbanded and no fewer than 13 strikes. A new union was installed in 1992, and the facility has been strike-free since.

The plant has made dramatic improvements in quality. According to a 1992 quality audit by J. D. Power & Associates, Puebla was producing cars with an average of 226 things gone wrong (TGW) per 100 cars, nearly twice the industry average of 116 TGW. By 1996, that number had been cut to 95 TGW per 100 cars, only nine points above the industry average and less than half of the number from 1992. The goal is less than 65 per 100 by 1998, which would make the plant the best in its class.

Still, bugs can be expected in an all-new car like the Bug. A May 1998 recall to replace a battery tray that was rubbing against some wires affected all 10,000 New Beetles built. A new smaller tray was retrofitted at no cost to the owners. Other manufacturers, notably Saturn and Lexus, have overcome early recalls to post some of the best customer satisfaction numbers in the industry.

The New Beetle is built in a new final assembly hall. It is large, airy, and bright with white walls and huge skylights. It takes 2 1/2 hours for a painted New Beetle body to come in one door and leave the other as a complete car. That's about the same time it takes for one of the original Beetles in the next hall to be built even though the new car is a far more complicated piece of machinery. The difference is that the New Beetle is assembled from modules. Large components and subsystems like the dash come built-up from the suppliers, while the original Beetle, though simple, is practically hand-built by the assembly line workers. As a result, it is less labor intensive to build the New Beetle—only 2,000 of the plant's 15,000 workers are assigned to the new car. At peak production, the goal is to produce 500 New Beetles a day. The Mexican plant is responsible for

ABOVE AND OPPOSITE
From the start, a convertible has been part of the Concept 1 project. The cabriolet, shown at the 1994 Geneva Motor Show, is not likely to go into production anytime soon. *Volkswagen*

building the engines, while the transmissions are shipped in from Germany. VW indicates that over 70 percent of the car's content comes from North American suppliers, who also maintain inspectors in the plant to assure high quality.

The final leg in Volkswagen's strategy to keep the New Beetle fresh in the minds of consumers will be to continually upgrade the car with new features and options. The first change will be the introduction by early 1999 of a higher perform-ance model boasting a five-valve, 1.8-liter, tur-bocharged, four-cylinder engine. In addition to producing 150 horsepower at 5,700 rpm and 155 foot-pounds of torque at 4,600 rpm, the turbo

model has larger 17-inch wheels and a unique pop-up spoiler located at the top edge of the rear window. At speeds above 40 miles per hour the spoiler extends to give the car additional stability. VW estimates that the 1.8 Turbo will be capable of going from 0–60 miles per hour in 9.0 seconds and will have a top speed of 125 miles per hour.

During a test at Ehra-Lessien, journalists who drove the 1.8 Turbo gave it an enthusiastic thumbs up. It has the snap lacking in the nor-mally aspirated 2.0-liter four and literally runs circles around the turbo-diesel. The 1.8 Turbo will be for New Beetle aficionados what the GTI was to the Golf.

Piëch also stressed that since the New Beetle shares its underpinnings with the new Golf, just about any technology that appears on that model can easily be adapted to the Beetle. This means that an all-wheel-drive syncro, a five-speed automatic with Tiptronic manual shifting, or even VW's legendary 190-horsepower VR6 may soon be on tap.

What about a convertible? Piëch, who was so overwhelmed by the reception of the Concept 1 in Detroit, immediately ordered up a cabriolet, red with a white interior to pay homage to the Swiss flag, for the Geneva Show two months later. Freeman Thomas said that while the Simi Valley design studio had only seven weeks to build the car, it was a task for which they were well prepared.

"We had already done studies in the studio for what a cabrio would look like," Thomas said. "If you look at the cabrio, it's very clear it does not look like an afterthought because it was never an afterthought. It was part of the original concept. In fact, it makes a much more clear statement than the original Beetle cabrio because of the way the windows line up with the rear deck lid. Also, when the roof is up, it has the exact same look as the coupe."

But Simi Valley had other ideas about Piëch's red and white design scheme. "We didn't want to paint this car red on the outside and do the interior in white—that would have been the obvious thing to do," Thomas recalled. "What we wanted to do was to choose the correct color. Part of the process was that we wanted a color that was

Hold the anchovies. Bacino's, a Chicago pizzeria, ordered up four specially painted New Beetles as delivery vehicles. *Tirerack*

modern, at the same time it was soft and friendly and had a technical feel to it. When we started on the combination for Geneva, we decided we wanted a softer, more waxy red, very technical. And when we did the interior, we did most of it in a charcoal, and we found almost a basketweave leather cloth. The car came off being sophisticated. Piëch loved it."

So a convertible is probable, but not in the short term. With the New Beetle a virtual sell-out, there is little incentive for the additional investment in a production version of the convertible. So in the meantime, those looking for an open air experience will have to content

themselves with the glass sunroof or seek out aftermarket converters who will chop the top off a standard model. As sales of the New Beetle eventually slow, as they do when supply catches and passes demand, additional capacity will be freed. Only then will a convertible be tooled up. Since no one knows how long the current round of Beetlemania will last, no one can say when the cabriolet will be needed. Piëch merely says on the convertible question, "For the moment, not yet," and smiles.

So what's beyond the New Beetle? A Microbus revival? "What about it?" Freeman Thomas coyly retorts. Then again, that's another story.

Herbie lives! It didn't take long for the Neumann Automotive Group, a Southern California aftermarket specialist, to customize one of the first New Beetles. *Neumann Automotive Group*

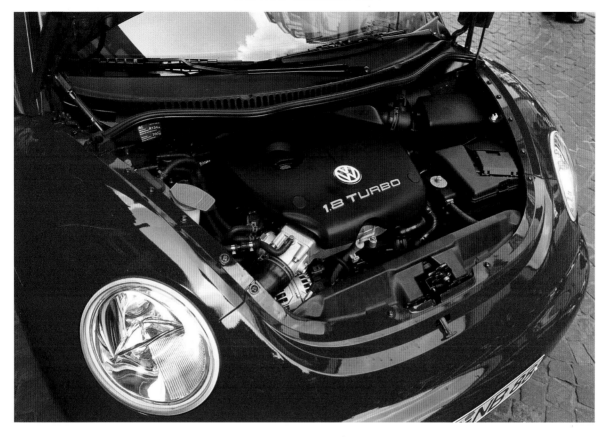

Coming in January 1999 is the much-anticipated 150-horsepower, 1.8-liter gas turbo. *Jim Fets*

OPPOSITE
The higher performance Turbo models are distinguished by a pop-up spoiler mounted at the top of the rear window. *Jim Fets*

NEXT
A New Beetle meets the original in the Alps' Grossglockner Pass. *Jim Fets*

CONCEPT 1 TECHNICAL DATA

Vehicle Dimension

Length (inches)	150.5
Width (inches)	64.4
Height (inches)	59.0
Wheelbase (inches)	99.4
Weight (pounds)	1,995
Track F/R (inches)	58.5/58.5
Overhang F/R (inches)	26.1/25.0
Ground Clearance F/R (inches)	7.0/9.4

POWERTRAINS

	TDI Version	Electric Version	Hybrid Version TDI Motor	E-Motor
Engine/Motor				
Type	Direct-Injection Diesel (4 cylinder)	AC Induction	Direct Injection Diesel (3 cylinder)	AC Induction
Displacement (cc)	1,900	n/a	1,400	n/a
Max. Power (hp)	88	50	67	24
Max. Torque (lb-fts)	148	96	103	n/a
Transmission	5-speed "Ecomatic"	2-speed Automatic	5-speed Semi-Automatic	–
Motor Location	Front	Front	Front	Front
Battery				
Battery Type	–	Na/NiC1*	–	Ni/MeH**
Battery Weight (lbs)	–	572	–	396
Stored Energy (kW)	–	22	–	10
Rated Capacity (Ah)	–	90	–	55
Off-Load Voltage (v)	–	248	–	180

*Na/NiCl: Sodium/Nickel Chloride
**Ni/Meh: Nickel/Metal Hydride

Performance Data				
Max. Speed (mph)	112	77	102	65
Fuel Consumption (mpg)	46.7	–	132.4	
Electric-Range (miles) (Urban Driving)	–	94	–	–
Electric-Range (miles) (Constant Speed: 30 mph)	–	155	–	65
Acceleration (0–62 mph)	12.8 seconds	n/a	n/a	n/a

1998 U.S. NEW BEETLE TECHNICAL SPECIFICATIONS

Engine:

	Gasoline		Diesel	
Type	2.0l, 4-cylinder, in-line		1.9l, 4-cylinder, in-line	
Bore (inches)	3.253.13			
Stroke (inches)	3.653.76			
Displacement (in³)	121.1	1984 cm³	115.7	1896
Compression Ratio	10.0:1		19.5:1	
Horsepower (SAE) @ rpm	115 @ 5,200 (85 kW @ 5,200)		90 @ 3,750 (66 kW @3,750)	
Max. torque, lbs-ft @ rpm	122 @ 2,600 (165 Nm @ 2,600)		149 @ 1,900 (202 Nm @ 1,900)	
Fuel Requirement	Regular unleaded		Diesel	

Engine Design:

Arrangement	Front mounted, transverse
Cylinder Block	Cast iron
Crank Shaft	Cast iron, 5 main bearings
Cylinder Head	Aluminum alloy, cross flow
Valve Train	Single overhead camshaft, spur belt driven, 2 valves per cylinder, maintenance free hydraulic lifters
Cooling System	Water cooled, water pump, cross flow radiator, thermostatically controlled electric 2-speed radiator fan
Lubrication	Rotary gear pump, intermediate shaft driven, oil cooler
Fuel/Air Supply	Sequential multi-port fuel injection (Motronic)
Emissions System	OBD ll, 3-way catalytic converter with 2 oxygen sensors (upstream and downstream), enhanced evaporation system

Electrical System:

Alternator, Volts / Amps	14 / 90
Battery, Volts (Amp Hrs)	12 (60)
Ignition	Digital electronic with knock sensor
Firing Order	1-3-4-2

Drive Train:

Configuration	Front-wheel drive

Transmission Gear Ratios	5-Speed Manual		4-Speed Automatic	
	Gasoline	Diesel	Gasoline	Diesel
1st	3.78:1	3.78:1	2.71:1	2.71:1
2nd	2.12:1	2.12:1	1.55:1	1.44:1
3rd	1.36:1	1.36:1	1.00:1	1.00:1
4th	1.03:1	0.97:1	0.68:1	0.74:1
5th	0.84:1	0.76:1		
Reverse	3.60:1	3.60:1	2.11:1	2.88:1
Final Drive	4.24:1	3.39:1	4.88:1	3.71:1

Capacities:

Engine Oil (with filter) (quarts)	4.8
Fuel Tank (gallons)	14.5
Cooling System (quarts)	6.7

Steering:

Type	Rack and pinion, power assisted
Turning Circle (curb to curb) (feet)	35.4
Ratio	17.8:1

Interior Volume—SAE: 96.3 (ft³)

EPA Class   Subcompact

		EPA
Passenger Volume (ft³)	84.3	84
Trunk Volume (ft³)	12.0	12
Seating Capacity	Four	

	Front	Rear
Volume (ft³)	49.7	34.6
Head Room (inches)	41.3	36.7
Shoulder Room (inches)	52.8	49.4
Leg Room (inches)	39.4	33.0

Body, Chassis, and Suspension:

Type	Unitized construction, bolt-on front fenders
Front Suspension	Independent MacPherson struts, coil springs, telescopic shock absorbers, stabilizer bar
Rear Suspension	Independent torsion beam axle, coil springs, telescopic shock absorbers, stabilizer bar
Service Brakes	Power-assisted, dual diagonal circuits, 256-mm vented front discs and solid rear discs
Anti-Lock Braking System	Optional, all 4 wheels
Parking Brake	Mechanical, effective on rear wheels
Wheels	6-1/2 J x 16, steel, with full wheel covers, 5 bolts
Tires	205/55 R 16H all season
Drag Coefficient	0.38

Dimensions:

Wheelbase (inches)	98.9
Track: Front (inches)	59.6
Rear (inches)	58.7
Overall Length (inches)	161.1
Overall Width (inches)	67.9
Overall Height (inches)	59.5

	5-Speed Manual	4-Speed Automatic
Curb Weight (pounds)	2,712	2,778
Payload (pounds)	992	936

Fuel Consumption (EPA Estimates):

	5-Speed Manual		4-Speed Automatic	
	Gasoline	Diesel	Gasoline	Diesel
City (miles per gallon)	23	41	22	34
Highway (miles per gallon)	29	48	27	44

APPENDIX C

1998 U.S. NEW BEETLE STANDARD EQUIPMENT LIST

Legend:

● Standard, at no additional charge.   ■ Option, at additional charge.

◆ Part of option package, at additional package charge.

Technical

Brakes	Power-assisted front vented disc brakes, rear solid disc brakes	●
	ABS (anti-lock braking system)	■
Emissions	OBD ll	●
	50-state certification for gasoline and diesel engines	●
	TLEV (transitional low emissions vehicle) concept for California, and Massachusetts and New York only	●
Engine	2.0L 115 horsepower 4-cylinder, in-line, gas	●
	1.9L 90 horsepower 4-cylinder TDI, in-line, diesel	■
Side Impact	Anti-intrusion side door beams	●
	1998 U.S. Federal side impact compliance	●
Steering	Power-assisted rack-and-pinion steering	●
Suspension	Independent front McPherson struts	●
	Independent track correcting torsion beam rear axle	●
	Rear gas shock absorbers	●
Transmission	5-speed manual	●
	Clutch/starter interlock (car will not start if clutch is not depressed); manual transmission only	●
	Hydraulic clutch	●
	4-speed improved-efficiency (ETA) automatic, adaptive, with automatic shift lock	■

Exterior

Antenna	Roof-mounted, amplified	●
Brake Lights	Center high-mounted stop lamp (LED) in rear hatch under rear window	●
Bumpers	Body-color bumpers	●
Corrosion Protection	26-step paint/corrosion protection process	●
Doors	2 doors	●
	Door handles, body color	●
	Open door warning reflectors on lower door trim	●
Fender, Front	Plastic front fenders	●
Glass	Tinted glass	●
Horn	Dual tone horns	●

Lights, Front/Rear	Daytime Running Lights (DRL, upon start-up of vehicle headlights are engaged with reduced power, IP lighting, parking lights, and taillights remain off. To engage all lights with full power the light switch must be turned into "on" position.)	●
	Halogen projector beam headlamps with clear polycarbonate lens	●
	Halogen projector lens front foglamps	◆
Mirrors	Body-color mirror housings	●
	Driver & passenger side power mirrors, heatable	●
Moldings/Panels	Body-color rocker panel	●
Paint	Metallic Paint	●
Roof	Power glass sunroof, tilt and slide, tinted glass, with sunshade and power lock operated convenience closing feature (delayed introduction)	■
Tires	P205/55 R 16 H, all season tires	●
	Full size spare tire	●
Wheels/Covers	6-1/2 J x 16" steel wheels, black, with full wheel cover	●
	6-1/2 J x 16" alloy wheels–6-spoke, with VW logo hub cap and Anti-theft wheel locks	◆
Wipers/Washers	2-speed windshield wipers with variable intermittent wipe feature	●
Front	Heatable windshield washer nozzles (only in combination with heatable front seats)	◆

Interior

Air Conditioning	Air conditioning, CFC-free, with variable displacement A/C compressor	●
Alarm/Anti-theft	Anti-theft vehicle alarm system for doors, hood, trunk lid, radio, and starter interupt, with warning LED in drivers' door top sill and with activation "beep"	●
Ashtray	Dealer option	■
Assist Handles	Large assist handle in instrument panel above glove box, 2 rear passenger assist straps on b pillar	●
Center Console	(see storage, interior)	
Clock	Digital clock with blue display mounted in central forward headliner	
Cruise Control	Cruise control (effective at speed above 22 mph, 35 km/h)	◆
Cup Holders	(see storage, interior)	
Defroster	Electric rear-window defroster	●
Doors/Side Panels	Molded door trim in leatherette with upper sill molding in exterior body color (black on vehicles with white exterior)	●
	Integrated armrests in front door panels	●
	Integrated armrests in rear door/side panels	●
Floor mats	Front and rear carpet style, color coordinated	●
Fuel filler	Remote fuel filler release located on driver's door inner, flap connected to fuel filler neck to protect body	●

Instrument Cluster	Speedometer, tachometer, odometer, trip odometer, fuel gauge, gear indicator (if equipped with optional automatic transmission), warning lights	●
	Red illumination for controls (switches and buttons), blue illumination for displays (speedometer cluster and radio display)	●
	Headlights-on warning tone (upon opening of driver's door when ignition key is removed)	●
Keys	Valet key	●
Lighting	Combination interior and reading lamp located in bottom sill of rear view mirror with time delay	●
	Glove box light	●
	Luggage compartment light	●
Locks	Central power locking system (doors) with key-operated closing feature for optional sunroof (when available), opening & closing feature for power window (if so equipped) and selective unlocking at driver or front passenger door	●
	Door mounted lock/unlock switches for central locking system	●
	Radio-frequency remote locking system with lock, unlock, trunk release, and panic buttons on transmitter	●
Mirrors, Interior	Driver and front passenger visor vanity mirrors, illuminated with cover	●
Power Outlets	2 power outlets (SAE size) in center console	●
Radio/Audio	AM/FM cassette stereo sound system with control capability for (optional) CD changer, theft-deterrent warning light and coding system. 6 speakers: 2 tweeters in A-pillar, 2 mid-woofers in front doors, 2 mid-woofers in rear quarter trim	●
	CD-changer preparation (cable from radio to luggage compartment)	●
Restraint System	Driver and front passenger airbag supplemental restraint system	●
	Front 3-point safety belts	●
	Height adjustment for front 3-point safety belts	●
	Rear outboard 3-point safety belts	●
	ALR, ELR (automatic locking retractor, emergency locking retractor) for front passenger and rear outboard safety belts, to secure child seat in place under normal driving conditions	●
	Child seat tether anchorage system (rear seat)	●
	Emergency tensioning retractors for front safety belts	●
	Driver and front passenger side airbags	●
Seating, Front	Front seats, fully reclining, with height adjustment and "ring style" headrests	●
	"Easy entry system" integrated into front seat mechanism. Allows seat to move forward for easy access to rear seating area.	●
	Heatable front seats (only in combination with heatable windshield washer nozzles)	◆

Seating, Rear	One-piece folding rear seat	●
	Rear seat outboard "ring style" headrests	●
Steering Wheel	3-spoke padded steering wheel	●
	3-spoke padded leather wrapped steering wheel (only in combination with optional leather upholstery)	◆
	Height adjustable and telescoping steering column	●
	Steering wheel deformable upon impact	●
	Collapsible steering column	●
Storage, Interior	Front door storage nets	●
	Front passenger seatback magazine/storage pockets	●
	Glovebox, lockable with interior shelf	●
	Center console with 3 front beverage holders and rear concealed beverage holder, color coordinated	●
Trim (Details)	Leather wrapped steering wheel	◆
	Leather shift knob and boot (manual trans. only), and handbrake handle cover	◆
Trunk/Cargo Area	Luggage compartment carpeting on floor, left and right side, rear of seat back. Molded trim on trunk lid.	●
	Remote electric hatch/trunk release located on driver's door	●
Upholstery	"Primus" velour seat fabric	●
	Leatherette seat trim	◆
	Partial leather seat trim (seating surfaces)	◆
Ventilation System	Rear seat heat and A/C ducts, side window defoggers in IP	●
	Pollen / Odor filter for incoming air	●
Windows	Manually operated windows	●
	Power windows (simultaneous operation possible) with one-touch-up/one-touch-down features (with pinch protection) and convenience close & open feature (central locking operated)	◆

Warranty

	2 years / 24,000 mile New Vehicle Warranty	●
	2 years / 24,000 mile no-charge scheduled maintenance	●
	2 years unlimited mileage / distance 24-hour roadside assistance	●
	10 years / 100,000 mile Limited Powertrain Warranty	●
	12 year unlimited mileage Corrosion Perforation Warranty	●

INDEX